D1432429

Round Barns *of* New York

Round Barns *of* New York

RICHARD TRIUMPHO

SYRACUSE UNIVERSITY PRESS

First Edition 2004
04 05 06 07 08 09   6 5 4 3 2 1

Title page: Octagon barn, built around 1890, near Holland Patent, Oneida
County. Courtesy of the Preservation Center, Holland Patent Free Library.

The paper used in this publication meets the minimum requirements of
American National Standard for Information Sciences—Permanence of
Paper for Printed Library Materials, ANSI Z39.48-1984.∞™

Library of Congress Cataloging-in-Publication Data
Triumpho, Richard.
 Round barns of New York / Richard Triumpho.— 1. ed.
   p. cm.
 Includes bibliographical references and index.
 ISBN 0-8156-0796-2 (hardcover (cloth) : alk. paper)
 1. Barns—New York (State) 2. Round buildings—New York (State) I. Title.
NA8230.T75 2004
728'.922'09747—dc22   2004006285

Manufactured in the United States of America

For G. A. Garms

Richard Triumpho lives near St. Johnsville, New York, on the family dairy farm where he was born. He is a freelance writer, and for thirty years his regular column, "Jottings in a Dairyman's Journal," appeared twice a month in *Hoard's Dairyman* magazine, the Fort Atkinson, Wisconsin, publication known worldwide as "the bible of the dairy industry."

Triumpho is the author of two books, *No Richer Gift* (1980) and *Wait 'til the Cows Come Home: Farm Country Rambles with a New York Dairyman.* His articles have been published in *The Furrow, Agway Cooperator, Mohawk Valley USA,* New York State *Conservationist,* and *Country Extra.*

Contents

Illustrations

Donors

Susan Wilkinson Ferretti and Roger Ferretti

George Ann Garms

Mr. and Mrs. Willard Northrop

Alice Randel Pfeiffer

Valerie Voorhees

Foreword | Lowell J. Soike

A few weeks ago, when exploring a 1920s round barn that had gone unused for years, the scene easily drew me back in time. Stepping onto the barn's concrete floor, I stood near the wall and looked around. A silo in the barn's center rose up to the roof; between myself and the silo, a manure litter carrier rode on a circular track fixed to the ceiling, and in front of that stood a row of steel dairy cow stanchions. Nearly all the original equipment and fixtures—the ventilation system, hopper-type windows, and hardware—were still in place. The scene displayed a state-of-the-art experiment carried out during the era of horse and hand power. Quite obviously, round barns such as this were more than places to store hay, keep horses, or milk cows; in their day, they were technological marvels also designed with looks in mind.

Indeed, the farmers who built round barns, for all their variety, had one thing in common: they were all progressive in one way or another. In the last half of the nineteenth century, various wealthy "gentlemen" farmers built octagonal or many-sided barns for their stock farms, showing their interest in both improved agricultural practices and advanced rural building methods. Further innovations occurred during the early decades of the twentieth century; as agricultural prosperity and a rapidly changing dairy industry filled the rural air with optimism, many forward-thinking dairy farmers experimented with round barns designed with a silo in the center to more easily feed their herds. Others built round barns not from a commitment to new farming ideas or progressive agriculture, but because they enjoyed the notice they got from owning the first round barn in the neighborhood. Such a building gave a farmer, if nothing else, a talking piece for visitors and passersby, who marveled at the new kind of barn.

The primary fascination of round barns, now as then, lies in their unusual architecture. They stand out in rural places where we expect large buildings to be rectangular or square. This was especially true before the arrival of round silos, circular grain bins, and Harvestore manure slurry tanks.

But round barns also fascinate for what they suggest about their original owners. They remind us that those farmers who wanted one—always a minority—were demonstrating imagination, independence, and confidence. Such farmers first had to buck the opinions of their neighbors, likely to condemn them for exercising bad horse sense, putting on airs, or wasting time and money. But round barn owners stood their ground against neighbors who held to familiar, accepted views about the right way to build things, arguing that round barns provided a more efficient workplace than traditional designs, cost less in materials for the space enclosed, and were better able to withstand the winds that toppled so many other barns.

Round barns deserve to be remembered as well for the creativity of their carpenter-builders. Walking through one today, one cannot help but admire the skills shown by this breed of barn builders. The various round barn designs, indeed, gave these craftsmen a chance to showcase their woodworking talent. Able to calculate angles that many could not and to curve wood around a circular form, the innovative builders took pride in promoting this new kind of rural construction and in their association with it.

In fact, it was the builders themselves, more than the agricultural extension service engineers, who boosted the growth of round barns as they wrote in farm journals about the barns they had built and of their positive features. These builder-publicists, aided by willing farm journal editors, sought to grab the reader's eye by publishing illustrations of floor layouts and photos that showed their novel roof designs and complex framing. The results advertised themselves, spreading word of these innovative builders to other farmers wishing to have such barns.

With this book, Richard Triumpho explores how the ideas of round barns worked themselves out in an eastern state. The trends in New York departed from those of the Midwest, with its larger number of round barns. There eight out of ten round barns had been built after 1900, during prosperous times for Corn Belt farmers. Articles and books about the Midwest reinforced the perception of a movement there dominated by true-round "barrel" barns. But in New York, the pattern was different; nearly two-thirds of round barns built there were constructed before the turn of the century, resulting in a round barn tally dominated by octagonal and multisided varieties.

Underscoring this nineteenth-century construction "boom" is Triumpho's recognition of Elliot W. Stewart's important role in promoting octagon barns. A man of many talents, Stewart began work as a schoolteacher before becoming a lawyer in Buffalo. Energetic but physically frail, he retired from his law practice in 1853 at age thirty-six and moved a few miles southwest to his farm, near Lake View Station on the Lake Erie shore. There he continued to practice law as a sideline, set up a sawmill, and later started a summer camping resort on his farm. But his passion was pursuing farm improvements: he became a regular contributor to the *Country Gentleman* and other agricultural journals, published the book *Feeding Animals* in 1882, and served as a nonresident professor of agriculture at Cornell University. Meanwhile, Stewart undertook his most remarkable building project at his farm in 1875 when he replaced four small barns with a single large octagon barn. With the help of an experienced local builder, James Miller Claghorn, he drew up plans and erected an octagonal barn eighty feet in diameter, with a self-supporting roof. This unusual barn, promoted by Stewart in several articles, became a leading model for the merits of octagonal barns and stimulated a generation of innovative farmers to build octagons across the northern United States. Triumpho nicely details this history and points to New York examples that made use of the features urged by Stewart.

Stewart's enthusiasm for round barns is echoed by Richard Triumpho. In this fine book, Richard Triumpho faithfully records the history of this disappearing part of our rural architecture, vividly recounting the tale of their brief tenure as cutting edge rural design and allowing us to share his knowledge and enjoyment of round barns, and the place they had in this era of agricultural change and experimentation.

State Historical Society of Iowa
November 2000

Preface

Just five miles from our farm as the crow flies, near the hamlet of Fords Bush, two round barns always caught my eye as a youngster whenever my father drove that way. One was alongside the Fords Bush Road at the western edge of Montgomery County; the other was not far over the line in Herkimer County, on the Fords Bush Spur Road to Newville.

They seemed elegant and odd, so unlike the conventional dairy barns in our rural area, including my father's, which were all built on the plan of the Pennsylvania barn of the mid-1800s: two-story rectangles with timber frames and gable roofs.

The two round barns were so astonishingly different, such prominent features of the landscape, that they were true landmarks. Both are now gone, though: one long since, the other, sadly neglected, taken down only a year ago. It seemed wrong that they should fade away "unwept, unhonored, and unsung." So a while ago, in the spring of 1992, I decided to see how many of these fine old barns were left in New York State, to photograph them and write down the bit of history about each that could be gleaned from the present owners. Little did I know that my quest would take me far afield—into New England and Canada, down the Atlantic Coast to Georgia, and through the Midwest clear to the Pacific—for the story of round barns is woven throughout North America.

One of my leads put me in touch with Larry T. Jost of St. Louis, Missouri, who had compiled a list of 180 round and polygonal barns in Wisconsin for a course in cultural geography at Carroll College in Waukesha, Wisconsin. His research also provided him with records of twenty-nine barns in New York State and forty-six in Vermont.[1]

With this information in hand, I began taking day trips to photograph the New York barns. Most of them were within a few hours' drive of my farm in the Mohawk Valley. After morning milking and an early breakfast I would point my pickup south into Otsego, Schoharie, and Delaware Counties and still manage to be home for evening milking at six o'clock. Later, as I ventured into New England, the photo trips became weekend excursions; a part-time herdsman tended chores in my absence.

Aside from occasional magazine articles, published research on round barns is limited. Early on, when I visited Donald Martin, owner of the McArthur barn in Delaware County, he loaned me a copy of William L. Wells's *Barns in the U.S.A.*[2] This book spurred my interest. Later, when my first magazine articles on round barns appeared in print, I received several letters from readers throughout the United States, who sent information, photos, and newspaper clippings about barns in their localities.[3] One correspondent brought to my attention Lowell Soike's fine book, *Without Right Angles: The Round Barns of Iowa.*[4] Soike's book introduced me to Elliott W. Stewart—farmer, professor, and editor—who built New York State's first octagon barn in 1874 and led the campaign to promote the octagon barn in other states.

After visiting all the round and polygonal barn sites in New York State, interviewing the current owners, and researching many agricultural publications, I discovered I had collected enough material to write a book. So I gathered my photos and notes and began.

Acknowledgments

This book would not have reached completion without the generous sharing of knowledge granted me by many other barn enthusiasts. Much valuable information was furnished by Mark Peckham at the New York State Office of Parks, Recreation, and Historic Preservation, who provided a copy of the Central Plan Dairy Barns of New York Thematic Resources Survey he completed in 1984 in collaboration with Mark Reinberger. Lowell J. Soike's pioneering work on the round barns of Iowa was another tremendous help. Thanks goes also to Larry T. Jost, who generously supplied leads to many round and polygonal barns in New York State.

Deserving praise for their assistance are these town and county historians: Shelby Mattice, for taking time from her busy schedule to provide special access to the Bronck barn; Mary S. Dibble, for sharing her records of the Nobbs barn; Bonnie Shumway and Lowell Newvine, for information on the Oswego County barns; Mary Ann Kane, for researching Sid Sautelle's history; Beverly Tyler, for sending information and photos of the Stony Brook barn; and Cheryl Delano, for ferreting out old records of Elliott Stewart.

The following individuals likewise merit enduring thanks for their significant contributions: Mercy Nobbs Warren, Bob Bates, Nancy Northrop, Donald Martin, Varick Stringham, Jr., Warren Wigsten, Harold Berry, Jr., Jim Berry, Blair Fraiser, Albert Anderson, Lynwood Hand, Ed Schultz, Dorothy Goodrich, Donald O. Cook, and Mrs. Howard Jantzi.

Round Barns *of* New York

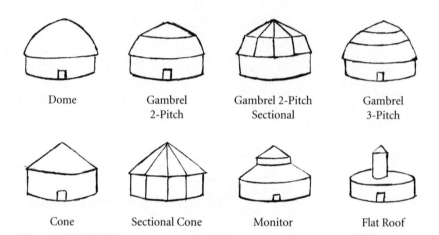

Dome	Gambrel 2-Pitch	Gambrel 2-Pitch Sectional	Gambrel 3-Pitch
Cone	Sectional Cone	Monitor	Flat Roof

1. Roof shapes. Drawing by Richard Triumpho.

1 | A Different Barn

As you drive south from Albany on Route 9W and pass a few miles below the village of Coxsackie, keep looking off to the right side of the highway and you will see a handsome red barn of unusual shape. A round barn! So startlingly different from its neighboring rectangular barns is this crimson beauty that you turn off the highway to admire it. A sign identifies it as the Bronck barn, built in the 1830s. Closer scrutiny reveals that the barn is not truly round like a barrel, but in fact has thirteen sides, which gives it a circular configuration.

Circular barns like this one are rare indeed on New York farmsteads. Less than one-tenth of one percent of New York farms ever had one. Research could document a total of only forty-three having been built in this state, but undoubtedly others existed that were never recorded and now are lost to historical memory. Who built these barns, and why?

Although nearly every state has at least one or two of these barns, most were built in the Midwest. Nearly 1,000 were built in just five states: 170 in Iowa, 170 in Minnesota, 155 in Illinois, 215 in Wisconsin, and 226 in Indiana.[1]

New York's total of forty-three round barns puts it far down the list. Nevertheless, New York holds a prominent place in the round barn era, for it was a New York State native, Elliott W. Stewart, whose zealous writings in the agricultural press about the merits of octagon barns brought the circular concept to the attention of progressive farmers not only in the Empire State but in the Midwest as well. Stewart's influential articles appeared at the same time the Midwest farm economy was booming and post-Civil War prosperity was fostering a surge in all types of barn building. This circumstance accounts for the great number of octagon barns built in America's heartland.[2]

Relatively reliable dates have been determined for most of these New York barns, beginning with the c. 1815 nine-sided carriage barn in Allegany

County and ending with the 1950 completion of the Voorhees barn in Montgomery County.

With the exception of three pre-Stewart-influenced barns (the c. 1815 Allegany County nonagon, the c. 1860 Livingston County octagon, and the c. 1866 Chautauqua County dodecagon), the barns can be grouped into three chronological types. This is the system used in 1984 during the "Central Plan Dairy Barns of New York State Thematic Resources Survey" conducted by Mark Peckham of the New York State Division of Historic Preservation and Mark Reinberger, at that time a graduate student at Cornell University.

The first chronological type, barns built from 1874 through the early 1890s, includes octagon barns with heavy timber framing, a stone-walled basement containing rows of stanchions in straight lines, and hay storage on upper floors.

In the second type, exemplified by two barns built in 1883 and 1896, Peckham and Reinberger noted the trend to more efficient internal configuration: a large ground-to-roof haymow dominates the center of the barn, and the hay is circled by a ring of stanchions on the ground floor and a wagon drive on the upper floors.

In the third chronological type, which were built from 1893 to 1950, the Thematic Resources Survey recognized the final development of the centralized form: the central haystack has been replaced by a round, central silo; and heavy timber post-and-beam framing has been replaced by light "dimension lumber" framing.[3]

By detailing the events in the chronology of barn building and design, I hope to shed additional light on the little-understood history of farm architecture in New York State.

Geographic Distribution

Round barns were built in only twenty-nine of New York's sixty-two counties. The barns are scattered throughout the state, with most being located in traditional dairying areas: the Hudson, Mohawk, Delaware, and Chenango river valleys; the Finger Lakes region; the eastern floodplain of Lake Erie; the floodplain south and east of Lake Ontario.

Nine of the counties had more than one round barn: Cortland, Erie, and Montgomery County had four of these barns; Chenango, Delaware, Dutchess, Oswego, Otsego, and St. Lawrence each had two; the remaining twenty counties had one each.

By definition, a barn is a farm structure for sheltering and feeding animals, and/or storing farm crops and equipment. In New York, thirty-three round or polygonal barns were built specifically for sheltering animals; ten were built for equipment storage or related uses giving the total of forty-three.

A further breakdown of the thirty-three animal barns shows that one sheltered sheep, another pigs; one housed circus animals; one was built for horses in Adirondack lumbering country; and the majority, twenty-nine, were built for dairy cows.

The ten remaining barns served a variety of uses related to either animals or farm equipment. Five were exhibition halls for agricultural products at fairgrounds, three were carriage barns, one was a training arena for circus animals, and one was an office at a chicken farm.

Terminology

The word "round" has gained acceptance as a generic term for barns of circular shape whether truly round like a barrel or polygonal with five or more sides of equal length.[4] The overlap of usage can be confusing. However, the barn lover will agree that, as Eric Arthur and Dudley Witney point out, "all the dramatic architectural qualities to be found in the circular barn will be discovered also in the polygonal and . . . the more sides to a barn, the greater the difficulty, visually, in distinguishing one form from the other."[5] To avoid ambiguity, when each barn is taken up for individual discussion in this book, I will use specific nomenclature for the polygonal barns: octagon, nonagon, dodecagon or twelve-sided, thirteen-sided, fifteen-sided, sixteen-sided. Only the truly barrel-shaped barns will be called round. Certain other definitions are also necessary.

Timber frame construction refers to heavy post-and-beam timbers (essentially hewn tree trunks) fitted together with mortise-and-tenon joints secured by wooden pegs.

Balloon frame construction means the entire building skeleton is made with a series of closely spaced vertical studs—2" x 4" or 2" x 6" sawed lumber—nailed to both the first-floor sill and the wall plate to support the weight of the upper floors and roof, thus completely eliminating heavy timbers.[6]

A *bank barn* has part of the foundation wall against a hillside, making a split-level barn: the basement or cow stable opens out to the lower ground level and the haymow on the upper floor opens out to the upper ground level, making it easier for the horse team to pull hay wagons into the loft. When no hillside was available, a *ramp barn* was built. Dirt was hauled to make a ramp sloping up almost to the hayloft door; then a short bridge of planks connected the ramp to hayloft floor.

Barns had various kinds of external sheathing, notably *board and batten, clapboard,* and *shiplap.* Board and batten is sheathing formed of boards nailed vertically, with joints between boards covered by *battens*—narrow strips of wood nailed along the joint of two upright boards, to make the joint weatherproof. In this context, a *board* refers to a length of sawed lumber six to twelve inches wide and one inch or less thick. Clapboard is formed by nailing boards in successive horizontal rows, beginning at the *sill* (bottom) of a wall and proceeding up to the top plate under the eaves, with each succeeding course of boards overlapping the course below it by about an inch to form a weatherproof siding. Shiplap sheathing is similar to clapboards, with one major difference: by having the long edge of the boards cut away for a portion of the width (about $1/2$ inch) on both edges, but on opposite sides, so that succeeding courses of boards fit together with flush joints, forming weatherproof siding.

A *bent* is the basic framework of a timber frame building, which, depending on the building's width, consists of two to four upright posts connected by horizontal tie beams.

Roof construction involved certain other specialized elements. A *purlin* is a longitudinal beam supporting the rafters and positioned midway between the eaves and the roof ridge. It is in turn supported by vertical *purlin posts.* A *squinch* is a short plank, or lintel, carried across the corner of a wall to support a superimposed mass, such as roof rafters.

In the description of roof types, the traditional terms *gable* and *gambrel* as applied to rectangular barns were used by Roger Welsch to describe Nebraska round and polygonal barn roofs. In applying these terms to the unusual barn configurations, he defined the barn roofs on the basis of silhouette: if the rafters ran straight up from the wall plate to the central peak, forming an inverted cone, he called this a gable roof (even though there was no gable); if the rafters sloped up from the wall at one angle, then bent and continued at a flatter angle to the center peak, he labeled it a gambrel roof.[7]

Lowell J. Soike applies Welsch's definition of gambrel to the roofs of Iowa round barns; however, he uses the terms *conical* and *sectional cone* instead of gable.[8] Soike's terms seem more accurate and will be used in this discussion.

Finally, barn interiors often included a *haymow,* which was an upper floor or loft used for storing hay. The main floor might be divided into *stalls,* small pens or enclosures for livestock. Each cow might also have a *stanchion,* a yoke made of a pair of upright planks or pipes designed to secure her neck during milking or feeding. Stanchions were usually built in parallel rows for a herd of cows, with an manger in front.

New York's barns represent all phases of development for round barns, with the central plan barn being continuously reinvented and refined during its half-century of popularity. The barns were built during a period of unprecedented agricultural prosperity and growth, when farmers welcomed new ideas. Inventions like Cyrus McCormick's grain reaper and John Deere's steel moldboard plow were accelerating farm progress, and new laws passed by Congress in 1862 were beginning to transform American agriculture. The Homestead Act and the act chartering the Union Pacific Railroad opened up western lands; the Morrill Land Grant College Act encouraged agricultural education; and the act establishing the Department of Agriculture assisted farmers in adopting scientific methods. As Alfred Stefferud put it in *Farmer's World: The Yearbook of Agriculture,* "The coming together of various lines of technology, the emphasis on agricultural reform, and the profitability of agriculture created an agricultural revolution."[9]

Round and polygonal barns were built during those exciting and innovative years. Architecturally they rank with the finest examples of vernacular construction, and their beauty is astonishing. The winds of change have not been kind to them, however, and the relentless march of progress has passed them by. New styles of prefabricated farm buildings, devoid of the beauty of the old handcrafted barns and created to meet the needs of new technology, dominate the rural landscape. Yet in our rush toward ever-newer technology, we should not forget what those old barns represent: the cutting edge of an earlier time when progressive farmers searched for ways to apply scientific methods and industrial ingenuity to animal husbandry.

The word *vernacular* originally was used to describe the spoken, native language of a region, to distinguish it from a literary or scholarly language. Architectural historians borrowed the term to describe buildings that were not "high style," not designed by professional architects. Farm buildings—barns in particular—have long been ignored by art historians as not being legitimate American architecture. Exotic though round and polygonal barns seem, it would be a mistake to dismiss their emergence on the rural landscape as just a passing fad or flight of whimsy by a few eccentric farmers. They are an important part of our cultural past, lonely reminders of an earlier generation of agricultural visionaries who strove to make the farm workplace more efficient and economical.[10]

A Barn Primer

The significance of the round barn era to American agriculture can be better appreciated when one has an acquaintance with the early history of our traditional barns, their European roots, and how barns worked in nineteenth—and beginning twentieth-century America.

From time immemorial, farmers have lived in close contact with their animals. The barn has a venerable lineage traced back more than two thousand years to the Saxon house/barn in Europe, which had barn, cow stable, and house under one roof. The floor plan of that ancient dwelling for both man and beast was a prototype of what eventually came to be called *basilican*. It was rectangular in form, with a large, oblong central space known by historians as the *nave* and a gallery on each side forming an *aisle*. The nave was the threshing floor, and the aisles had stalls for animals—cows, horses, pigs, and sheep. Above the stalls was a loft, or *mezzanine*, where men and women farm workers slept on the hay and sheaves of grain stored there. The entrance to this barn was a wide door at one end of the threshing floor. Inside, at the further end of the threshing floor, were the household cupboards and, in a low pit, the cooking fire.[11]

The threshing floor has been an integral part of barns since antiquity. Threshing itself is an occupation recorded even in the days of the Egyptian pharaohs. It involves separating the kernels of grain from the stalks by beating the stalks with a flail and then winnowing the grain to separate the kernels from the chaff. Sometimes the ripened sheaves were spread on the floor, or even on packed ground, and oxen made to walk upon them to tread out the grain. Our word *threshold* dates from Saxon times when the "goodman," upon entering the barn, had to cross the *therscold* or threshing floor to reach his living area; thence came its current meaning of "the sill of a doorway."

The three styles of barns brought to the New World by the early settlers from Europe used the basilican plan, with one major difference: the barn was built separate from the house. The barn was vital to the survival of the farmer and his family, ensuring that their most valuable possessions—their tools, animals, and animal feed—were sheltered, so it was built before the house itself, and the family lived in a rude cabin the first few years.[12]

One of the earliest types of barns in North America was built by Dutch immigrants who settled the Hudson, Schoharie, and Mohawk River regions in the seventeenth and eighteenth centuries. In New York State it is known as the Dutch barn, and it is a direct descendant of the Dutch barn of the Netherlands. The Dutch barn varies slightly from the basilican plan in that it

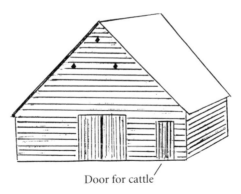

Door for cattle

2. Barn styles: The Dutch barn in North America was nearly square in shape, with a steep roof and low eaves. Doors on both gable ends opened to the threshing floor, allowing wind blowing through the barn to help disperse chaff when winnowing grain. The barn siding consisted of horizontal clapboards and the roof of wooden shingles. Drawing by Richard Triumpho.

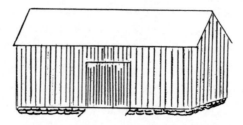

3. Barn styles: The English, three bay, or Connecticut barn was about thirty feet wide by sixty feet long. A central pair of doors on the long side of the barn, front and back, opened to the threshing floor or driveway, with a bay or *mow* (rhymes with *cow*) on either side. Siding consisted of verticle boards and the roof of wooden shingles. In later years, to add a dairy, this single-story barn was jacked up and a stone-walled stable built underneath. Drawing by Richard Triumpho.

is somewhat wider than it is long, and it has wagon doors at both gable ends. Again we see the nave as a threshing floor, and the aisles as cattle stalls. The nave is separated from the aisles by tall timbers spaced at regular intervals forming bays; the timbers in turn support the steep roof. A low ceiling over the threshing floor and cattle stalls also serves as the floor of the loft, or mow, where hay and other fodder required by cattle in winter is stored.[13]

A second type of barn brought to the New World from Europe came to

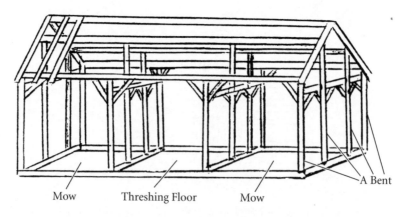

Mow   Threshing Floor   Mow   A Bent

4. This drawing shows the frame of an English barn, which is divided into three bays by four *bents*. Each bent is an assembly of four upright posts with cross braces, formed of large timbers (8" x 8" or 10" x 10"), their mortise and tenon joints held securely with *trenails* (wooden pegs). Drawing by Richard Triumpho.

be known as the three-bay or English barn. It differed from the Dutch barn principally by having a wagon door entrance to the threshing floor on the long sidewall.[14] This sturdy, single-story barn usually measured thirty feet wide by sixty feet long and flourished in the early to middle 1800s when wheat was the dominant crop. After 1850, when the agricultural economy shifted from wheat to livestock, the English barn changed to accommodate animals. Sometimes a stable was added at one end, giving the barn greater length. Another solution was to jack up the frame and build a stable under it, the walls of the stable being constructed of mortared stone.

The third type of barn is the two-level or Pennsylvania barn, and the dominant groups influencing its architecture were Swiss and German immigrants.[15] This generally is a bank barn, built against the side of a hill, so that access to the second-story wagon doors from the hillside is fairly level. Where the terrain is flat, an earthen ramp is built to the upper story. The ground floor of the Pennsylvania barn is the stable for horses, cattle, and oxen; the upper story holds the hayloft and threshing floor (which also serves as a storage area for farm machinery during the winter.)

In the late 1800s a new structure, the silo, became a familiar addition to the Pennsylvania-style barn. During those years dairying emerged as an im-

5. Barn styles: The Pennsylvania barn is a two-story "bank barn," built into a hillside to allow level access to the threshing floor driveway, to make it easier for the team hauling hay wagons to the mow. When no hillside was available, a ramp of dirth was built to the haymow driveway. The timber frame is similar to that of the English barn, but the Pennsylvania barn shows German and Swiss influence in its *forebay,* a projection of the upper story intended to protect the lower-story windows and doors from rain and to serve as a shelter when harnessing horses. Drawing by Richard Triumpho.

portant part of the farm economy, and agriculturists explored better ways of feeding animals to extend milk production through the winter. A major innovation was the silo, a circular structure in which green feed such as chopped corn plants could be preserved by its own fermentation, much as sauerkraut is preserved in an earthenware crock. The resulting product—silage—made a succulent winter feed. The silo is a tall cylinder, twelve to eighteen feet in diameter and anywhere from thirty to seventy feet high, constructed of wood or concrete staves or steel.

Throughout the 1700s and 1800s, all the work of feeding farm livestock in the barn involved hand labor. In summer, hay harvested in the meadow was pitched by hand onto wagons, hauled by draft animals to the barn's threshing floor, and pitched off into the mows on either side. In winter the hay was forked by hand from the loft down to the stable twice a day to feed the livestock. Likewise, the corn silage stored in the silo was forked out by hand daily and carried to the cattle in baskets or wheelbarrows. All this involved many steps, much walking back and forth, and many long lines of travel.

And if these chores weren't enough, one of the end products of all this feeding—manure—had to be shoveled away by hand. So it is easy to understand that a major concern of farmers in that era was eliminating as many needless steps as possible. Eventually, the search for efficiency in caring for livestock led some agricultural innovators to consider the concept of a round barn. Hopefully the following pages will bring the reader a new awareness of how significant these distinctive barns are to New York State's agricultural heritage.

2 | Rounding Up Origins

"In few vernacular buildings," comment Eric Arthur and Dudley Whitney, "do the dramatic effects of space and colour, of height and depth unfold as they do in the circular barn with aisle." [1]

Where did the idea for America's round barns originate? Some hint might be gained from Larry Jost's summary of the history of the architecture of circular buildings in the United States in *The Round and Five-or-More Equal-Sided Barns of Wisconsin*. The earliest such buildings were Dutch octagonal churches in New York; at least twenty were built in the Hudson Valley before 1750. Another possible European antecedent of the round barn concept was a type of agricultural building found in the northern counties of England in the late 1700s, the gin-gang, defined by Jost as "a small and often round or octagonal building near the barn which housed the threshing machine's driving gear and the horse which powered it."

Another circular farm building found in England was the hay rick, a wooden frame for drying hay. Although its invention has been attributed to Lovell Edgeworth in the mid-1700s, it appears that hay ricks have been found in Holland since the 1500s. Use of hay ricks in the American colonies, where they are called hay barracks, dates to the 1700s in New Jersey. According to Jost, "Hay was stored in the upper barrack level, and cows were housed beneath." [2]

Eric Arthur and Dudley Witney, while claiming to find no historical evidence of circular barns in Europe, did point out that the circular plan in house construction goes back to Britain's Bronze Age people who used rough boulders to build their round houses. [3] They also say that the builders of circular barns may have been inspired by the round churches and baptistries built in Europe in the early Christian and Medieval periods. [4]

John Hanou turned up a book dealing with vernacular architecture in rural France. It contains a drawing of an octagonal barn with a thatch roof, included in a plate illustrating "Barns of Normandy." Details of the barn's construction or location could not be determined.[5] Other researchers wrote that precedents could be traced as far back as the plan for St. Gall Monastery, made in A.D. 800 which shows a circular farm structure probably intended as a poultry house.[6]

America's First Circular Barn

The first circular building used strictly for agricultural purposes in the United States was a sixteen-sided barn built in 1793 by George Washington on his Dogue Run Farm in Fairfax County, Virginia. He wanted a place to thresh wheat indoors, out of the weather. What he essentially did was build a "treading circle" of planks and construct a barn around it.

He not only thought up the concept, he drafted the plans himself in New York City during his first term as president and sent the plans to his farm manager with the directive that he had finally "resolved to build a Barn and treading floor at Dogue Run Plantation."[7]

6. In 1793, George Washington built this sixteen-sided barn on his Dogue Run Farm to thresh wheat. The barn was destroyed by fire in 1967. Courtesy of the Mount Vernon Ladies Association.

The barn's diameter of fifty-two feet gave ample space for a treading circle for oxen or horses to trample the wheat from the straw. He placed the planks about one inch apart; this allowed the threshed kernels to fall through the gaps to the basement granary where they were bagged and stored.

Washington was a progressive farmer searching for crops to replace the plantation's tobacco-monoculture trade with England. He had enough vision to realize that the plantation's single crop of tobacco, based on trade with the mother country and subject to the whims of British merchants and markets, was not sustainable agriculture; it not only wore out the soil, it was unprofitable and outmoded for the new nation.[8] He abandoned tobacco for a novel idea: intense cultivation of grain, particularly wheat. The innovative circular barn was designed for his new venture into grain farming.

In addition to being a revolutionary soldier and statesman, Washington was a revolutionary farmer, a leading agronomist of his time. He carried on extensive correspondence about farming methods with Thomas Jefferson, with leading agriculturists in England, and subscribed to English farm journals. Witty Sanford thinks it may have been a 1790s English publication discussing the feasibility of polygonal farm forms that influenced Washington to build his hexadecagon barn.[9]

Washington's barn did not survive the ravages of time. It burned in 1967. Its crumbled brick walls then became part of a foundation under a housing subdivision down the Potomac from Mount Vernon. The barn plans, however, did survive, and it was from these plans, written in his precise surveyor's hand, that an exact replica of the barn was built in 1996 at Mount Vernon. (When Washington built his 1793 barn he was faced with a farmer's traditional cash-flow squeeze. He instructed his nephew to barter fish for the planks, nails, and shingles for the barn. What a difference 200 years makes: the 1996 replica cost $1.8 million to build!)[10]

George Washington, progressive farmer, exemplifies a major theme of this book: America's unique round barn concept was the work of forward-thinking, multitalented agricultural leaders willing to try new ideas, including new architectural forms, to incorporate new economies and technologies with the changing needs of farming.

Soon after Washington built his sixteen-sided barn, a true-round brick

7. This replica of George Washington's barn, shown under construction in March 1996, was dedicated on September 27, 1996. Photograph by Richard Triumpho, 1996.

barn was built nearby in Keswick, Virginia.[11] No record exists of any other circular barns being built during the ensuing twenty years.

Then in 1824 a splendid central plan dairy barn was built by the Shakers in Hancock, Massachusetts.

The sect known as the United Society of Believers in Christ's Second Appearing originated in England during a Quaker revival. The name Shakers was given to them in ridicule because of the violent dancing and leaping that accompanied their early religious services. The founder of the sect in America was Mother Ann Lee, who immigrated in 1774 with her husband and seven followers. The colony they started in Watervliet, New York, in 1776 became the parent Shaker community in America and attracted many converts.

In addition to agriculture, the Shakers engaged in manufacturing, becoming known for their practical inventions and particularly their furniture, which combined simplicity with durability. The barn built by the Shaker community at Hancock demonstrated their inventiveness and craftsmanship. The Shakers held the circle to be the most exemplary form of creation; some believe that idea influenced them to build a true-round barn.[12]

8. With the windows of the clerestory illuminating the high central space of the loft, the interior of this 1824 Shaker barn in Hancock, Massachusetts, is even more dramatic than the exterior. Photograph by Richard Triumpho, 1993.

The barn burned down in 1865, but it was rebuilt on the same foundation and its fame increased. It was huge, ninety feet in diameter, with stone walls thirty inches thick. The Shakers, always innovative and efficient, designed the barn as a feeding system to stanchion fifty-two cows in a circle on the ground floor, heads facing in toward the haymow, which was an open-sided central tower fifty-five feet wide and thirty feet high. This system allowed hay to be pitched out and fed with a minimum of steps.

In rebuilding, the Shakers improved on the original design by putting trapdoors in the gutter behind the stalls so that manure could be scraped and dropped down to manure wagons below in the barn basement. For better ventilation, and to aid the curing of hay, in the center of the mow they built an octagonal ventilating shaft that terminates above the roof in a cupola with windows on all eight sides.

The master stroke of their superb ingenuity was adding a twelve-sided clerestory to bring even more light to the interior. The whole arrangement was a model of efficiency and strikingly beautiful as well. Eric Arthur and

9. Leonard Bronck's thirteen-sided barn, built around 1832, may have been patterned after the Shaker barn just twenty-five miles to the east, across the Hudson River. Photograph by Richard Triumpho, 1993.

Dudley Witney conclude, "Like all great architecture, its interior is inseparable from the exterior and is, if anything, even more dramatic."[13]

The Bronck Barn

The design of the original 1824 Shaker barn was given wide circulation in agricultural journals.[14] It may have influenced Leonard Bronck, Jr., a few years later (about 1832) to build what was probably the first circular barn in New York State. Bronck, the sixth-generation descendant of Swedish settler Jonas Bronck (for whom the Bronx was named), built a thirteen-sided timber barn three stories high on his dairy farm near the west bank of the Hudson River at Coxsackie, just twenty-five miles from the Shaker village at Hancock, Massachusetts.

The Bronck structure, like the Shakers', was basically a haystack with a barn built around it. However, unlike the Shaker barn, it was strictly for hay storage; a rectangular addition housed the cattle.

The barn, seventy feet in diameter, has thirteen timber frame panels on a partially below-grade, mortared stone foundation; each panel is composed

10. Detail of the Bronck barn framing, showing a corner squinch. Photograph by Richard Triumpho, 1999.

of eight-inch-square posts with corner braces and four-inch-square studs. The panels are tied together at the top plates by squinches bolted through the plates at each of the thirteen corners; this forms a stiff ring to support the base of the thirteen triangular roof panels.

The roof panels are eight-inch-square rafters connected by four eight-inch-square purlins. The original wood shingles have been replaced by asphalt shingles. This thirteen-section hipped roof is topped by an octagonal cupola with louvers. In the center of the barn, a round pole nine inches in diameter rises from the ground to the apex of the roof. Although this pole is not necessary to support the roof, it may have been used to raise the barn.

11. The interior of the Bronck barn is completely open and was used as a big circular haystack. Photograph courtesy of the Bronck Museum, 1963.

12. The exterior of the Bronck barn. Photograph courtesy of the Bronck Museum, 1963.

The barn has a clapboard exterior. Internally it is completely open in plan, with a dirt floor below grade and a wood-plank drive floor at grade along the west side of the mow from which hay wagons were unloaded.

An original rectangular wing on the northwest side of the barn was removed some years ago; the square opening in the mortared stone foundation where it was attached has been filled with concrete. The barn apparently was designed to house the dairy herd in the rectangular wing and store hay in the circular portion.

A preliminary plan for the barn, dated 1832, has handwritten calculations of its volume; this indicates Bronck's desire for efficiency in enclosing maximum hay storage capacity with a minimal amount of lumber.[15]

The Octagon Fad [16]

The Shakers were not the only ones to consider nature's most perfect shape to be the circle. Orson Squire Fowler, a New York phrenology enthusiast and editor of the *Phrenological Journal,* also embraced the circular form.

Fowler was born and grew up in Cohocton, New York, where he worked on his father's farm. Perhaps these early years at the drudgery of farm chores led him to think of more efficient ways to handle work. At any rate, he en-

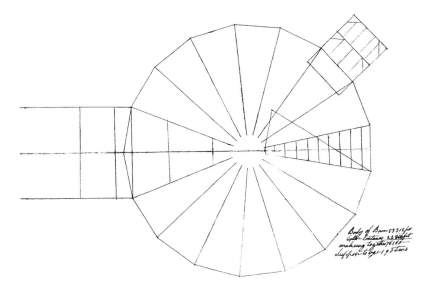

13. An 1832 pencil drawing of the plan for Leonard Bronck's barn, with hand-written calculations of its volume. Courtesy of the Greene County Historical Society.

tered Amherst College wanting to become a minister but became attracted to phrenology.

In 1850 he began a crusade for the octagon plan as being the ideal shape for a home. He believed everyone could be his or her own architect if "they were endowed with strong phrenological characteristics of a love of home and an ability to build." [17] Perhaps the mysticism used in studying human character from the shape of the skull led him to believe that living in an octagon house would change people's character, rendering adults and their children "constitutionally amiable and good." Welsch calls him "one of those curious combinations of genius and eccentric that season America's history." [18]

14. Leonard Bronck's signature, from his 1832 pencil drawing of the plan for his barn. Courtesy of the Greene County Historical Society.

Fowler described many advantages of the octagon shape, the major one being its efficiency in requiring fewer materials to enclose the same amount of space as a rectangle. While the circle was the absolute best in that respect, he believed the octagon had an advantage in being easier to build.

Fowler expounded his theory in an 1854 book, *A Home for All, or The Gravel Wall and Octagon Mode of Building.* This volume was even more successful than his first book: *Amativeness, or Evils and Remedies of Excessive Sexuality,* which went through forty printings. Both books had immense influence.[19]

His ideas caught fire, prompting hundreds of octagon houses to be built throughout the country between 1854 and 1860. In New York State alone, 125 octagon structures were built.[20]

Although Fowler's book printed no actual barn plans, he described the ideal farmstead as having an octagon house and octagon barn. The barn would be a two-story building with a ramp to the second-story haymow. He went into considerable detail in his discussion of barn interior arrangement to save steps and ease chores. He was particularly pleased that the center of an octagon barn was the proper shape for threshing with either horses or a flail.

Historians disagree as to whether Fowler's books and public tours influenced circular barn building. Soike thinks not, since "unlike octagon houses, no barns can be traced directly to him." He adds that "farm journals had ceased any mention of Fowler by the early 1860s. His cause, with respect to barn architecture at least, evidently died aborning."[21] Welsch, on the other hand, believed that, given the phrenologist's enormous popularity, "It is certainly likely that Fowler's influence on sophisticated house architecture spread also to popular barn construction."[22]

An anomaly because of its shape and very early date (c. 1815) is a nonagon brick carriage barn in Allegany County. This nine-sided barn was built on the Church-Bromeley Belvidere farm in Belvidere soon after construction of the main house was begun in 1804. Daniel Fink notes, "The main house was built by Philip Church, the first owner and Alexander Hamilton's nephew; its design is attributed to Benjamin Latrobe, the well-known Philadelphia architect."[23]

Although the Church-Bromeley farm buildings were erected in the wilderness, a sophistication in construction is evident in the fact that the bricks for the polygonal carriage barn were made on location and some of the corner bricks were made to shape, whereas common brick would have required cutting for the corners of the polygon. Framing of the second-story floor joists was done without posts, leaving the ground floor completely free of any obstruction to the storage and turning of carriages.[24]

A Livingston County Octagon Barn

In 1987, when Daniel Fink finished seven years of research on *Barns of the Genesee Country, 1790–1915* and published his book, this octagon barn was still standing on Coe Road in the town of Livonia. He measured the sides as being fifteen feet long, and took the accompanying photograph. He described the barn as being sheathed in board and batten and said it was difficult to tell if there had once been a cupola because the barn had been

15. This octagon barn was built about 1860 on Coe Road near Livonia in Livingston County. Photograph by Daniel Fink, 1985.

recooked. The roof was a sectional cone of eight panels. He was unable to provide further information other than estimating the construction date as being approximately 1860.[25]

When I visited the site in August 1999, the barn was a heap of fallen lumber. The roof had caved in, and four of the walls that hadn't already collapsed were leaning precariously inward against the ruins of the roof boards. The wall panels showed that it was of heavy timber frame construction, which supports the estimated 1860s date of construction.

A Twelve-Sided Barn in Chautauqua County

An anomaly because of its shape and early date was the twelve-sided barn along U.S. Route 20 about a mile east of the village of Westfield in Chautauqua County. The barn was built in 1866 by a Mr. Blowers who came from Cuba, New York, and used it as a dairy barn. Although it is near the home of Elliott Stewart, whose certain influence over octagon barn design will be discussed in the next chapter, it predates Stewart's barn by eight years. It remained in the Blowers family until 1942.[26]

It was a two-story timber frame barn with the sills resting on large fieldstones. The siding was board and batten. A gable-roofed rectangular wing

16. This twelve-sided barn, belonging to Alfred Nobbs, was built in Chautauqua County in 1866. Photograph by Donna Eisenstadt, 1979.

led to the huge, high hayloft. Stanchions on the ground floor were in straight rows along the walls. A heavy pole in the center of the barn rose from the ground through the second floor and held a diamond-shaped purlin to support the rafters. The roof was a twelve-section cone of moderate pitch, and it had a twelve-sided cupola topped by a spire.[27]

The barn also had a second rectangular wing that originally was attached to the house. That wing was later moved to another part of the property where it served as a tenant house. An aerial photograph taken in 1962 shows the barn still had a cupola at that time. The exact date it was removed could not be determined.[28]

Alfred Nobbs purchased the farm in 1945 and used the barn to store grape baskets for his vineyard. He said that many people in the county had been interested in preserving the barn, but they had been unable to secure the funds to restore it. The barn deteriorated and was torn down around 1990.[29]

3 | A Flurry of Octagons

Elliott W. Stewart has been credited with creating the "fad" for octagon barn construction that spread from New York State into Pennsylvania and across the Midwest in the 1880s.[1] He was born July 14, 1817, in Georgetown, Madison County, New York, where his father had settled upon moving from Bennington, Vermont. After graduating from Cazenovia Seminary, he taught school in Camden, Oneida County; at the same time he tutored private pupils preparing for college and began reading law. He was admitted to the bar and began practice in Buffalo in 1846, continuing until ill health forced him to relinquish his practice to his partners.[2]

In 1853, he and his wife purchased 209 acres of land close to Eighteen Mile Creek near Lake View in Erie County, New York. According to a newspaper article of the time, "Here Mr. Stewart became both a 'gentleman' farmer and a very practical 'dirt' farmer. Moreover, in fact, he became a 'Farmer of the (then) Future', since he not only improved established farm methods, but initiated new techniques as well."[3]

In 1874, fire destroyed four barns on his farm. He hired a carpenter,

17. Elliott Stewart, college professor and editor. Stewart promoted the octagon barn in leading agricultural journals during the 1870s and 1880s. As a result of his influence, many octagon barns were built in the Midwest as well as in New York. Photograph from *The Town of Evans Sesqui-Centennial* booklet. Not dated.

James Miller Claghorn, to replace the ruined structures with a single barn of unconventional form: an octagon. Where he got the idea for this radical departure from traditional barn architecture has never come to light. Undoubtedly he was aware of the Shaker round barn in Hancock, Massachusetts, which had been rebuilt just a few years earlier after a similar barn fire. Farm journals in New York had published many articles about the numerous advantages of the unique Shaker design, and its fame had spread far and wide. So it would be not unreasonable to assume that Stewart was inspired by the Shaker example.

When Stewart's barn was completed in 1875, he was so proud of his accomplishment that he wanted farmers everywhere to hear of his barn's superior design. Moreover, he had the ways and means to spread his gospel. Not only was he a respected farmer in the Empire State, he had just been appointed a nonresident professor in principles of agriculture at Cornell University, and he was also editor of a monthly paper, the Buffalo *Livestock Journal.* He prepared an article, complete with engravings of his barn, for the January 1876 issue of the journal, commenting, "Our 4 barns . . . covered about 7,000 sq. ft., while this 'octagon', 80 feet in diameter, encloses only 5,350 sq. ft. and yet has a capacity much greater than the 4 barns enclosing the larger area." Moreover, the space in his new barn was more usable.[4]

The article attracted a great deal of interest; readers wrote to editor Stewart requesting copies of his barn plan. Two of New York State's leading agricultural journals, the *Cultivator and Country Gentleman* of Albany and the *American Agriculturist* of New York City, reprinted the article in their summer issues of 1875. The *Illustrated Annual Register of Rural Affairs* volume of 1878 (published by the *Cultivator and Country Gentleman*) also reprinted the article with updated details by Stewart. When another reprint appeared that same year in the *National Livestock Journal* (based in Chicago), the editor commented that reader response continued unabated and that applications for reprints of the barn plan "continue to come in, in considerable numbers." In 1883, Stewart included the article in his new book, *Feeding Animals.*[5]

All this publicity certainly helped promote the octagon barn. By 1884 Stewart could write approvingly that "some 30 or 40 have been built in various parts of the country—among them five in Pennsylvania, three in Indiana, four or five in Illinois, two in Minnesota and several in Kentucky." [6]

After Stewart's Buffalo journal was absorbed by the *National Livestock Journal* of Chicago, Stewart himself continued the campaign by serving as a corresponding editorial expert on octagon barns for D. D. T. Moore's *Rural New Yorker* and other national farm journals. [7]

Stewart's timber frame octagon barn, eighty feet in diameter, was two stories high. The internal configuration was rectangular on the ground floor, where there were two parallel rows of wood stanchion stalls for forty cows with their heads facing a center aisle feed manger. These two rows were flanked by two driveways for manure disposal. Contained within the parallel rows of stanchions was a grid of beams and supporting posts for the upper floor. A row of stalls for six horses was against the south wall; against the opposite wall were pens for calves and bins for storage of roots and other items. [8]

Stewart enumerated the advantages of the octagon barn over the rectangular barn. Octagon barns were cheaper to build because they enclosed more storage capacity than rectangular barns having the same wall height. The short lengths of the eight wall sections required no long timbers for

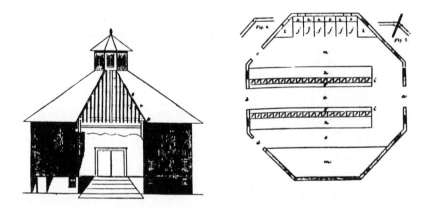

18. The ground-floor plan of Stewart's barn, built in 1875, featured a rectangular configuration with parallel rows of stanchions. The second-story loft was open because the self-supporting roof needed no interior posts. Courtesy of the New York State Division of Historical Preservation.

framing. Even though a true-round barn could hold slightly more than an octagon, he pointed out that "the true circle is too expensive to build and the octagon approaches the circle in economy of outside walls, and is as easy to build as the square."[9]

Stewart stressed the convenience of combining all farm activity in one building rather than scattered around the farmyard in several smaller barns. Another big advantage was the barn's self-supporting roof: its rafters rested only on the outside walls of the barn, unlike the rectangular barn's roof, which needed interior posts and purlins. Thus, the octagon barn's haymow, being wide-open space, was more easily filled by the new rope-and-pulley horse-drawn hayfork that could run unobstructed on a circular track to any spot. The roof itself was cheaper to build because, as Stewart explained, "The economy of footage is exhibited strongly by comparison of my 4 barns with the 'Octagon' that takes their place . . . 100,000 shingles were required to roof the former, while 60,000 covered the 'Octagon.' "[10]

In those nonmechanized times, all chores in the barn required handwork and repetitious walking back and forth. Stewart pointed out a significant labor-saving feature of the octagon: "Barns that are square or circular have shorter lines of travel than the oblong form." And Stewart had a clincher, his argument for the octagon's superiority over its rectangular cousin: "The octagon or sixteen-sided form is much less affected by the wind and may be built higher than the long barn in windy situations."[11]

Shortly after completing the octagon barn, Stewart constructed a smaller octagon barn to serve as the farm workshop. In this building he perfected several labor-saving inventions: "self-cleaning" stable units for cows that were sold and shipped in large numbers throughout the United States, and a "cow tail-holder," patented February 2, 1875. This device was a metal "bracelet" that held the cow's tail switch firmly to its lower left leg, safeguarding the person milking the cow from being swatted in the face by the tail. According to Donald D. Cook, the Town of Evans historian, "the cow tail-holder met with instant success . . . so many orders were received at the farm that Mr. Stewart was obliged to make arrangements with Pratt and Company of Buffalo, N.Y., and Hoard and Worden of Jamestown, N.Y., to manufacture these 'Bovine Bracelets.' "[12]

Stewart's enthusiastic campaign obviously influenced other New York farmers to adopt his design. Thirteen octagon barns have been identified with reliable construction dates from the 1870s through the 1890s. Undoubtedly, many others were built in the state during that time interval but never documented.

The Baker Octagon Barn

On a hillside west of Canadarago Lake in Otsego County is one of the earliest known octagon barns still surviving in fine condition in New York State. It continued to function as a dairy barn for more than one hundred years after its construction.

The barn is sixty feet in diameter, three stories high, and has a sectional cone roof topped by an octagonal cupola with eight windows. It was built in 1882 by Norman, Herbert, and H. N. Baker and was probably designed by them, closely following the plan of Elliott Stewart's octagon barn that was printed in the July 1876 issue of the *American Agriculturist.* The fieldstone

19. The Baker barn was built in 1882 by Norman, Herbert, and H. N. Baker. This view shows all three stories. The bottom entrance opens into the cow stable. Photograph by Richard Triumpho, 1993.

foundation walls with rough quoins are said to be the work of a mason named R. O'Brien.[13]

The first two stories have these fieldstone walls; the third-story walls are timber frame covered with vertical board siding. The heavy timber frame consists of 8" x 8" posts at the corners and midpoints of each side, with 6" x 8" top plates. These wall frames also have diagonal wind bracing. Across the top plates of each of the eight corners, frames are tied with squinch blocks, creating a stiff continuous ring to support the outward thrust of the roof. The roof is an eight-panel cone. It is framed with 4" x 6" beams at the sides and center of each panel, and with 3" x 6" rafters in between. The original roof covering has been replaced with asphalt shingles.

The roof shows one significant variation from Stewart's model: it is not self-supporting. A center square of four posts rises from the ground floor up through all the stories to the cupola, giving intermediate support to the rafters. Stewart's roof was entirely self-supporting, leaving the hayloft completely open, devoid of posts. Apparently the builders were not completely

20. The roof of the Baker barn was not self-supporting. A square of four posts extended from the ground up through all three stories. Photograph by Richard Triumpho, 1993.

comfortable with Stewart's design and added the four posts as an extra margin of safety.

The barn shows another interesting departure from the model: it has three stories, whereas Stewart's had only two levels. In Stewart's barn, threshing was done in the center of the unobstructed hayloft. The Bakers added another intermediate loft for threshing.

They fit the barn against the hillside so that each of the three levels has entrance doors to the outside. The ground-floor cow stable entrance faces south; the second floor has large entrance doors east and west; the third-floor entrance bay faces north. Using the space below the north entrance bay is a storage room on the second floor and a square silo on the ground floor. This silo was an innovation at the time and was mentioned in an 1886 article on the barn.[14]

On the southeast side of the octagon barn is a rectangular gable-roofed addition, three stories high, with access to all three stories of the main barn. The ground story of this addition was used for machinery storage, the upper stories for hay.

21. The Bakers built their barn against the hillside, allowing ground-level access to all three stories. Photograph by Richard Triumpho, 1999.

22. The layout of ground floor in the Baker barn was almost identical to that of Stewart's barn, with parallel rows of stanchions. In the far wall is the entrance to the stone silo. Photograph by Richard Triumpho, 1993.

The cow stable on the ground floor of the octagon has a plan almost identical to Stewart's. There are four parallel rows of stanchions. The two inside rows face a center aisle that services their mangers; the two outside rows face the outer aisles. Two intermediate aisles contain the gutters. The floor is concrete.

The cow stable framing is 8" x 8" posts spaced at irregular intervals in the stanchion rows. These posts support heavy beams upon which lay the joists of the second floor, which are mostly logs six inches in diameter. The second-story framing is similar to the ground story except that the joists are heavier, rough logs ten inches in diameter. Both the second and third stories have board flooring.

In 1984 at the time of the Central Plan Dairy Barns of New York State Thematic Resources Survey, the Baker barn still housed dairy cattle. When I visited the farm six years later, the cows were gone, the dairy operation had gone out of business, and the barn was empty except for a forage harvester stored in the loft. At the time of this writing in August 1999, the barn remains empty but is still in remarkably good condition, attesting to the

23. The Baker barn has a horse stairway connecting the first and second floors. Photograph by Richard Triumpho, 1999.

craftsmanship of its builders in the nineteenth century and the concern of the present owners who keep the roof weather tight.

The Lunn-Musser Octagon Barn

Also in Otsego County, and located less than twenty miles southwest of the Baker barn, is another early example in New York State of the octagon barn plan promoted by Elliott Stewart; it was built in 1885 by William Lunn on his farm in the township of Lisbon. The barn is on the south side of County Road 16, not much more than a mile southeast of the hamlet of Garrattsville in rolling country that once had many small-scale family dairy farms.

Evidently the Baker octagon, built only three years earlier, had a definite influence on William Lunn, for he copied many of the structural variations Baker incorporated. These include the center square of posts supporting cupola and roof and diagonal wind bracing on the wall panels.[15]

The Lunn-Musser barn is a two-story octagon sixty feet in diameter. It was built with a sectional cone roof of eight panels, originally topped by an octagonal cupola that blew off during a windstorm in 1976 and was not replaced.

The first-story walls are mortared fieldstone. A marble date stone, en-

24. The Lunn octagon barn, built in 1885, was still standing in 1993.
Photograph by Richard Triumpho, 1993.

graved "Wm. Lunn 1885," in the foundation wall attests to the pride the owner had in his new barn. A second marble date stone was removed in 1953–54 when a concrete block rectangular wing was joined to the southeast side to add more stanchions.

The framing of the upper-story walls was identical to that of the Baker barn, including diagonal bracing and squinch blocks. The roof framing had

25. Pride of ownership is shown in this marble date stone on the Lunn barn. Photograph by Richard Triumpho, 1993.

26. The Lunn barn as seen in 1999 shows the fate of many of New York State's round barns. Photograph by Richard Triumpho, 1999.

slightly different dimension lumber, being framed with 3" x 10" hip rafters with 3" x 8" rafters in between; it had wood shingles. The ground-story main entrance, originally on the west side, was moved to the southeast addition. A ramp on the northeast leads to the upper story.

27. A view from the stable of the rectangular addition to the Lunn barn shows a fallen beam after the roof collapsed onto the hayloft floor. Photograph by Richard Triumpho, 1999.

The ground-floor stanchion plan was changed to blend with the new addition, but it appears to have been similar to the Baker arrangement originally.

Again like the Baker barn, at the time of the 1984 Central Plan Dairy Barns of New York State Thematic Resources Survey, this was still a functioning dairy farm operated by Alex Musser. However, when I visited the barn eight years later, it was empty and the house vacant.

Apparently under a heavy snow load during the winter of 1996, the roof caved in onto the hayloft floor. Another historic barn gone.

The Lattin-Crandall Octagon Barn

The Lattin-Crandall barn, built in 1893 in Schuyler County, is yet another historic representative of the octagon model championed by Elliott Stewart. Unlike both the Baker barn and the Lunn-Musser barn, which veered from

28. William Lattin had confidence in Stewart's self-supporting roof and followed his design in his own 1893 barn. Photograph by Richard Triumpho, 1999.

Stewart's plan by adding an intermediate support of four posts to help carry the roof, the Lattin-Crandall barn stuck faithfully to Stewart's self-supporting roof design.

William S. Lattin reportedly got the idea for his octagon barn from one he saw near Columbia Crossroads in Bradford County, Pennsylvania. The carpenter first hired for the construction "got cold feet" when he saw the unconventional design, so an all-around handyman-carpenter named George Stewart was brought in. He successfully completed the building.[16]

The barn is an octagon fifty-five feet in diameter and two stories high, with a sectional cone roof topped by an octagonal cupola containing eight windows. The barn siding is board and batten. At the west side a ramp leads to double, sliding wagon doors for the hayloft. A two-story gable-roofed rectangular addition is on the northeast.

The ground-floor stable is framed with heavy timbers on a stone foundation, log posts and beams supporting the joists. The stable has one straight row of stanchions and two horse stalls. The second-story framing is squared timbers. The hayloft on the second story has a center wagon drive flanked by large swing beams; the drive floor is heavy plank.

The farm was owned by the Lattins until 1946 when it was purchased by Lillian Wilkinson, a World War II widow who supported herself and three daughters by selling butter churned from her cows' milk. She later married Harley Crandall; they put the farmland in the Soil Bank and planted Christmas trees. Her daughter Sue Ferretti has happy memories of playing in the hayloft with her sisters. The farm is now owned by Marvin Lamos, who hopes to get a grant to help restore the barn.[17]

The Ephratah Octagon Barn

There is a record of one octagon barn in Fulton County. It was built on the farm located on Route 10 one mile south of Ephratah, where seven generations of Getmans resided after Frederick Getman came to America in 1710 and purchased six hundred acres of land in the Stone Arabia patent.

The barn was built for Levi Yauney in about 1880 and appears to have followed closely the plan of Elliott Stewart. It was a two-story timber frame on a stone foundation and had clapboard siding. The roof, like Stewart's

29. Dairy cows at milking time wending their way to the Ephratah octagon barn, built around 1880. Photograph from the collection of Alvin Berry. Date unknown.

barn, was a cone of eight pie-shaped wedges; it was topped by an octagonal cupola with louvers. The only windows were in the basement cow stable, which had a dirt floor and a plank platform for the cow stalls. The stanchions were in a parallel configuration.[18]

Access to the second story was by a ramp. This second floor was com-

30. Harold J. Berry, Jr., at the site of the Ephratah barn where he milked cows by hand during the 1940s. Photograph by Richard Triumpho, 1999.

pletely open in plan so that a wagon could be driven around the center. The haymows and granary were along the outer wall. A notable feature of this barn was the circular wooden track in the hayloft for unloading hay. Harold J. Berry, Jr., who worked on the farm as a boy and helped milk thirty-two cows by hand, told me there was a forty-foot-long ladder in the loft to reach the hay track, and that "Louie Van Valkenburg was the last man to climb the ladder to fix the hay fork car." [19]

The barn burned in 1948. The bicentennial book of the town of Ephratah has the following record: "An octagon barn built by Levi Yauney, which had been a landmark for years, burned August 4, 1948 with an estimated loss of $50,000. Mr. and Mrs. Howard Carpenter, who were away at the time, had made plans to purchase the farm October first. It was the largest barn in the area with storage capacity for 300 tons of hay and could house 70 cattle." [20]

The Hannibal Octagon Barn

In 1878 in Oswego County on the Lake Ontario floodplain, an imposing three-story octagon barn was built just west of the village of Hannibal. It was one of three octagon barns on the floodplain.

It also followed Elliott Stewart's plan but with the Baker variation of adding a third, or intermediate, story for threshing grain. It was a bank barn built by Orville Wiltse under the supervision of W. H. Lund. Hannibal town historian Lowell Newvine recalls that it was better than sixty-six feet in diameter. Each of the sides measured twenty-seven feet two inches.

The basement-story walls were fieldstone; the upper two stories were heavy timber frame with vertical siding. A large octagon cupola, twelve feet in diameter, crowned the sectional cone roof. [21]

There is no record of the plan of the ground-floor stable, but from the 1878 construction date it is safe to assume there was a parallel stanchion arrangement since other aspects of the barn followed Stewart's plan. A photograph dated May 1976 shows the barn still standing, but it burned down shortly thereafter. [22]

31. The Hannibal octagon barn, built in Oswego County in 1878, has a third intermediate story for threshing grain. Photo courtesy of Lowell C. Newvine, Hannibal town and village historian.

The Mexico Octagon Barn

A second octagon barn in Oswego County still stands in the town of Mexico. It was built as a sheep barn, complementing a larger dairy farm complex. Very little is known about who constructed the barn, but records in the Heritage Foundation of Oswego indicate that it was standing by 1880. The barn is thirty-five feet eight inches in diameter; each of the sides is fourteen feet in length. It has a sectional cone roof with no cupola. The building's position against a hillside provides level access to the second-story hayloft.

The foundation is fieldstone of various sizes. The basement story is a stable, divided by wide boards into several sheep pens. The upper story is timber frame. The rough sawed beams measure fourteen to fifteen inches in width and four to five inches in depth. Posts and beams are pegged with wooden pins. The original siding was vertical boards. They were covered

32. Sheep were housed in the ground story of this octagon
barn in the town of Mexico, dating from about 1880. Undated
photograph courtesy of the Heritage Foundation of Oswego.

with asphalt composition siding about 1950 by Earl Preman, who owned the
barn then.[23]

The barn is located about one-half mile south of the Mexico village line
on the east side of Ames Street.

A Niagara County Octagon Barn

Near the village of Ransomville in Niagara County, at 3339 Daniels Road, is
a small two-story octagon barn that was originally built to house pigs. No
information exists about the date of construction or the name of the builder
and original owner, but a list dated 1984 has Karl B. Wright as the owner at
that time.[24] The present owners are Mr. and Mrs. Graydon Krueger.

This barn is $33^1/_2$ feet in diameter and 30 feet high. The basement-story
walls are fieldstone and mortar; the basement floor is concrete and open in
plan, with a random arrangement of heavy posts and beams supporting the
joists of the upper story, which is timber frame. An earthen ramp leads to the
second story.

Each of the eight side wall panels of the upper story is thirteen feet eight

33. This handsome octagon barn near Ransomville, construction date unknown, was built for pigs. Photograph by Richard Triumpho, 1999.

inches in length with exterior siding of board and batten. This second story is also open in plan, and the flooring is random width plank. The roof is a sectional cone of eight panels. There is no cupola. The original wood shingle roofing has been replaced with asphalt shingles. The barn has been maintained in very good condition.

A Wayne County Octagon Barn

This 1880s octagon barn, still standing on Jenkins Road just west of the village of Red Creek, is an example of the influence of Orson Fowler's advice on the advantages of a bank barn.[25] It is a three-story bank barn, thirty feet in diameter, built by Burgess Jenkins.[26]

The basement-story walls are fieldstone masonry. The upper stories are timber frame covered in vertical board siding without battens. The roof is of very shallow pitch. The small octagonal cupola has louvers and a bell-shaped roof.

The bank setting provided a wagon drive to the second-story granary.

34. This 1880s octagon barn stands at Red Creek in Wayne County. Photograph by Daniel Fink, 1985.

The third-story hayloft had no ground level access; hay was hoisted by rope and pulley to a hay track that extended out through a doorway in the third-story wall.

The barn is now owned by Norman and Mildred Weeks; they want to keep it in good repair, but the cost of restoring the barn is more than they can afford. Mrs. Weeks said that the storms in the spring of 1999 broke some roof rafters, so the barn may not last much longer.

What a sad fate for such a handsome barn.

The Seneca Octagon Barn

An octagon barn was built sometime in the 1890s in the township of Seneca in Ontario County. It was located along U.S. Route 20 about five miles west of Geneva. Neither Seneca's nor Ontario County's historical societies have any written information on the barn, and no photograph could be turned up.

Rodney Lightfoot, who wrote a *History of the Town of Seneca,* said that as a youth he worked one summer in the barn at threshing time. He remembers being in the hayloft, pitching sheaves of wheat into the threshing machine. Lightfoot says that the barn was a timber frame of two stories, and the ground-story configuration had parallel rows of stanchions.

Lightfoot thinks the original owner of the farm was Charles Mosey and believes he had the barn built. The farm later was owned by Mosey's son-in-law, Drew Campbell. After Drew died, the farm was owned by an absentee landlord. Unfortunately the barn was allowed to deteriorate and was taken down sometime in the 1980s.[27]

A Long Island Octagon Barn

Suffolk County also has a late 1890s octagon barn located in Stony Brook. It was built by Silas W. Davis. According to the Three Village Historical Society,

35. This octagon house at Stony Brook was originally built as a barn in the late 1890s. Undated photo from *Three Village Guidebook*, courtesy of Beverly C. Tyler.

its construction "held together with wooden pegs is indicative of the area's large nineteenth-century ship building industry."[28] It is a timber frame, three stories high, and has an octagonal cupola with eight windows. The cupola has a wooden pinnacle. Cows were kept in the ground-story stable and carriages on the second floor.

In 1938 the barn was remodeled into a residence, at which time the board and batten siding was replaced with clapboards. In 1973 the clapboards were removed and the board and batten restored to reproduce the original appearance of the building. The present owner is Stephen Berenyi.[29]

Cortland County Octagon Barns

Cortland County had three octagon barns built in Homer; two were circus barns and one was a carriage barn. The carriage barn is at 26 Clinton Street behind the Northrop house, itself a magnificent white octagon built circa 1850 by Dr. Alphonso L. Head, a veterinarian. Both house and barn were built following Orson Fowler's design. After the gravel walls of the house were built, the wood from the forms was used to erect the carriage barn. The two-story carriage barn is timber frame, hewn chestnut, with a diameter of thirty-five feet and a height of forty feet to the octagon cupola. The roof is a self-supporting eight-section cone. Dr. Head used the carriage barn for his horses and as a veterinary clinic.[30]

The two circus barns were built by Sid Sautelle. This entrepreneur, born 1850 in Luzerne, New York, as George C. Satterlee, became in his twenties "Signor Sautelle" when he worked as a sideshowman for a circus in Connecticut. By 1882 he had his own circus with headquarters at Syracuse on the Erie Canal; every summer his circus floated from town to town on canal boats specially built to hold his wagons and animal cages.[31]

In 1890 he moved to Homer, and twelve years later he began two octagon barns as winter quarters for his circus animals. The larger octagon was a training ring; the smaller barn stabled the animals. Later he converted the larger octagon into a house for himself, his wife, and the circus people. Because of his wife's ill health, he sold his by-then famous three-ring circus to a brother-in-law of James A. Bailey of Barnum and Bailey.[32]

After Sid Sautelle died, the octagon house was converted to an appliance

36. The Northrup octagon carriage barn in Homer, built in 1850 by Dr. Alphonso L. Head, was used as his veterinary clinic, and also as a stable for his horses. Photograph by Richard Triumpho, 1999.

and farm machinery retail sales store, the Spencer Sales Company. The next owners, the Robinsons, turned it into a restaurant and bakery. At the present time, the octagon houses an antique business. The smaller octagon barn is no longer standing.[33]

As the photograph in chapter 8 shows, the former circus barn is a striking building with a dormer on each of the eight roof sections. The only other circular barn with this roof design that I have seen is a true-round barn located near State College, Pennsylvania. That barn has eight dormers on a triple-pitch gambrel roof. Could it be that its design was modeled on the octagon of Sid Sautelle, the entrepreneur who is now enshrined in the Circus Hall of Fame at Sarasota, Florida?

4 | Haystack Barns

Most of the variations on Elliott Stewart's model of the octagon barn did not change his ground-floor rectangular configuration of stanchions. While Stewart's plan did make for shorter lines of travel in feeding cows as compared to a traditional barn, some farmers searched for even more efficiency. They found it in a polygonal stanchion arrangement, where cows faced a circular haymow in the center of the barn. This plan had the big advantage of concentrating feeding chores in a core area: hay and grain, dropped from the hayloft through chutes directly in front of a circular manger, could be fed with an absolute minimum of steps. A concentric configuration, with a continuous circular gutter behind the cows, also allowed more efficient manure removal. Another advantage was a less awkward floor framing system. Stewart's octagon used grid framing on a centralized form; this produced irregular spacing of joists and awkward lumber cuts where the square grid met diagonal sides. A much better framing system resulted from the polygonal stanchion arrangement that gave a circle of posts from which the floor joists could run radially or concentrically. Peckham and Reinberger, in their 1984 survey, concluded that this major variation on Stewart's model was a significant step in the transition toward the fully integrated circular barns of the late 1890s and early 1900s.[1] Two examples of this chronological type were built in New York State.

The McArthur Sixteen-Sided Barn

The earliest of the two "haystack barns" was the McArthur sixteen-sided barn built in 1883 in the town of Kortright in Delaware County; its diameter of one hundred feet also ranks it as the largest polygonal barn in the state.

The design of this barn seems strongly influenced by the 1865 Shaker barn in Hancock, Massachusetts, where the cows in their stalls stood in a cir-

37. Aerial photo of Donald Martin's farm shows damaged roof section of McArthur barn. Photograph, 1984; photographer unknown.

cle with their heads facing the huge central haymow from which they were fed. John W. McArthur would certainly have been aware of the Shaker barn since it received wide coverage in agricultural journals.

McArthur designed a sixty-foot-wide haymow rising from the ground fifty feet through all three stories of his barn. On the ground floor, this haymow was surrounded by a circular feed aisle six feet wide; this aisle was surrounded by a circle of eighty stanchions—not a true circle, to be sure, but a sixteen-sided polygon (like the barn itself) with five stanchions in each of the sixteen segments. Cows in these stanchions stood on a platform of "cow beds" four and one-half feet wide (the cow beds forming another concentric ring) and they faced the haymow and aisle from which they were fed. Behind the cows was the outermost aisle, a circular barn floor eight feet wide used as a driveway.

On the two upper floors, the haymow was circled by an aisle twenty feet wide that served as a wagon drive for unloading hay into the mow. Both second and third floors had direct entrances from the hillside.

The barn was framed with heavy timbers, a third of them sawn from

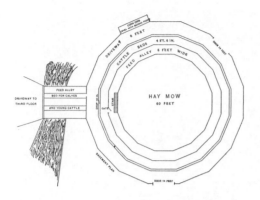

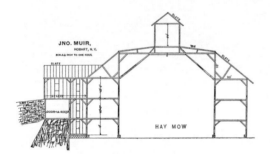

38. John Muir's plan and elevation for the McArthur barn, built in 1883. From "The Economic Barn," in *New Developments*, by John W. McArthur (Oneonta, N.Y: Oneonta Press, 1886), 129–42.

woods on the farm. Basic to the radial design was a polygonal ring of sixteen posts enclosing the mow. These posts were connected to sixteen posts at the exterior corners of the barn. The two rings of posts were tied together by beams, making sixteen bents, and the bents were connected by girders to form the main frame of the building. Posts and beams were mostly 8" x 10". Floor joists were logs eight inches in diameter, flattened on one side and spaced about three feet apart. The second-story floor was a double layer of one-inch boards; the third-story floor was two-inch plank.

The gambrel roof had two slopes, and the upper slope was relatively flat. Both slopes of the roof had a purlin at the center of their spans. The roof had board sheathing with slate on the lower slope and tin on the upper. A sixteen-sided cupola, twelve feet wide, was supported by a platform on top of tie beams across the tops of the inner circle of posts around the mow.

John W. McArthur described the design of this "Economic Barn" in his book, *New Developments,* and went into great detail about how much lumber was saved during construction as well as the convenience and work efficiency it offered in feeding and milking cows.[2]

McArthur's innovative ideas did not end when his barn construction was completed. He put together what was probably the first "milk pipeline" to convey milk from the stable to cooling cans in the milk storage room, which was one hundred feet away. This arrangement consisted of tin pipes (like roof rain gutters) in a circle around the outer aisle; milk poured through a funneled strainer into the pipe and flowed by gravity to the milk room, where it went through another strainer and into the cans. This eliminated carrying pails of milk back and forth to the milk room.

The number of steps saved—and arm muscles relieved—during each morning and evening milking session staggers the imagination (as I well know, since as a youngster one of my chores was to carry pails of milk). McArthur's barn was 100 feet in diameter with a circumference of about 315 feet. Rough calculation on the back of an envelope shows that to carry milk from his eighty cows required more than three miles of walking! The energy saved by this ingenious pipeline was very great indeed. Furthermore, his system was perfectly sanitary because the tin-pipe gutters had hinged covers to keep out stable dust, flies, and debris, and he stressed that "twice a day the covers are raised and the tin work thoroughly scalded and cleaned."[3]

McArthur's inquisitive and inventive mind made him virtually a Renaissance man of nineteenth-century agriculture. His book included, in addition to a description of his economic barn, a history of the newly formed Grange, "the first bold, decided and systematic step" in farmer organization; a treatise on the threat of artificial butter; and a broad range of articles, including "Co-operative Fire Insurance" and "Anti-Monopoly and Farmers' Alliance: The People Against Corporations," the latter expounding his views on the rise and power of corporate wealth, corporate bribery, and the farmers' alliance against corporate greed. His treatise on artificial butter demonstrates his early recognition of the danger to New York's dairy industry posed by this "spurious" imitation, masquerading under such names as oleomargarine, butterine, butteroid, creamine, and so on. "It has caused a great shrinkage in the price and value of dairy stock, and of land in dairy districts," he asserted soon after its introduction in the mid-1880s, "thus reducing the property of the farmers, who are engaged in a legitimate business."[4]

The saga of the McArthur barn echoes the story of most round barns: change of ownership through the years, difficulty in absorbing the expense of repairing the large roof because of a farm's negative cash flow during successive periods of declining milk prices and double-digit inflation, and finally failure of the roof followed by collapse of the remaining structure.

John W. McArthur died in 1914 at the age of seventy-four, thirty-one years after he built his barn. His widow sold the farm the following year to Frank Martin, who continued to milk cows there. Frank's sons Wendell and Lloyd took over the farm around 1925 after their father died. Wendell's son Donald became involved with the farm operation as he grew up; when Donald married in 1956, he and his wife, Juanita, went into partnership with Wendell and Lloyd. Ten years later Donald had enough equity to buy out his father and uncle, who were ready to retire.

In order to finance the mortgage, Donald Martin increased the herd size to ninety cows. The stalls in the round barn proved too small for the larger dairy cattle produced by selective breeding, so in 1969 a new free-stall barn and parlor were built for the milking herd. The round barn continued to be used for raising calves and replacement heifers. Double-digit inflation of the

39. The once-proud McArthur barn slowly sinking into the ground. Photograph by Richard Triumpho, 1993.

late 1970s and early 1980s made it increasingly difficult to service the debt of the new free-stall barn. Keeping up repair of the polygonal barn was out of the question. During this same period, the new milking parlor was plagued with electrical problems: stray voltage was causing increased mastitis and other herd health problems, which in turn were harming milk production and income, compounding the Martins' financial dilemma.

In 1958 a storm had damaged the cupola of the round barn. Rather than being replaced, the cupola was removed; it was thought to be too heavy for the rest of the roof anyway. In April 1983, a heavy, wet snowfall drifted to one side of the round barn's roof. "We were able to get up on the free-stall roof and shovel the snow off," said Donald Martin, "but there was no way to get up on the round barn roof to shovel that drifted pile of snow off. It just wasn't safe; with the cupola gone, there was nothing to tie a rope to hang on to." [5]

So that part of the roof collapsed under the snow load. An aerial photograph of the farm taken either in the fall of 1984 or the spring of 1985 shows the round barn roof with its collapsed section.

In 1984, the Erpf Catskill Cultural Center of Arkville, New York, considered restoring two historical round barns in the area: the Kelly true-round barn in Halcottsville or the McArthur hexadecagon. They opted for the Kelly barn. Nevertheless, they helped promote the McArthur barn for the National Register. People who visited the barn from the center suggested putting a tarpaulin over the hole in the roof.

"That wouldn't have helped save the rest of the roof," said Donald Martin, "and how could you have fastened a tarp on there to stay? What the roof needed was extensive repair, and we couldn't afford it." [6]

The fate of the barn was sealed. With the interior posts and beams exposed to the weather, it was only a matter of a few years before they began to rot, and the rest of the roof fell in, a section at a time. All that remains of this once magnificent piece of architecture are the outside walls enclosing the ruins.

The Hubbell-Parker Thirteen-Sided Barn

The Hubbell-Parker thirteen-sided barn in Schoharie County is the second transitional type that adopted the broad central haymow surrounded by a circular manger on the ground story and a circular wagon drive on the upper story. Dr. Richtmyer Hubbell built the barn in 1896 near the village of Jefferson. Although similar to the McArthur sixteen-sided barn located only fifteen miles south, it differs in one important aspect. The Hubbell-Parker barn uses light wood framing; this indicates a growing acceptance of the balloon framing techniques that became more and more popular after the Civil War.

The barn is on the south side of Route 10 on the eastern edge of the Jefferson village limits. It is two stories high and approximately sixty feet wide. It is on a level grade and is built of light wood framing with clapboard siding. Windows are in both stories of each of the thirteen sides. The gambrel roof is a two-pitch sectional cone with cedar shingles. It is crowned by a thirteen-sided cupola with louvers.

The barn has undergone various transitions in usage. In its first years it was a dairy barn. According to an article by Charles Hubbell, "It had four horse stalls and about 15 or 20 stanchions which was about all the farm could handle. One could drive all around the haymow and unload at any

40. One way to save a round barn: the Hubbell thirteen-sided barn, built in 1896 in Schoharie County, is now an antique shop. Photograph by Richard Triumpho, 1993.

side and then be able to drive out the doors that you had driven in a few minutes before."[7] Another owner converted it to a chicken barn. After that, it was used to raise veal calves. The barn is now owned by Bill Hubbell, who operates it as an antique shop.[8]

Because of these changes in its original function, the barn has been modified over the years. Several partitions have been built on the ground floor. On the second story, flooring was added to cover the central haymow. The ramp and bridge leading to the second story were removed in 1950.[9]

The basic structure has been left intact, however. Each of the thirteen wall sections is built of frames made of 2" x 4" studs and tripled 2" x 8" posts. Tripled 2" x 8" posts also form a ring around the former mow, extending upward to the break point in the gambrel roof. Beams for the upper floor radiate out from the center ring to the thirteen outer corners; these beams are made of half-round logs. Joists run between the beams, and the plank flooring is laid perpendicular to both the joists and the exterior wall. At the second story, a ring of breast girders circles the mow. The cupola is supported with 2" x 4" trusses. The barn has been maintained in good condition.

5 | Circles in Polygons

The "Plan of a Barn for a Dairy Farm" published in 1890 by Professor Franklin H. King contained radical features: a round barn of balloon framing and, in the center, an all-wood round silo.[1] Early research about the silage-making qualities of round silos was done by King, a physics professor at the University of Wisconsin Agricultural Experiment Station. In the 1880s, silos were still primitive structures, originally pits or vats, in which forage crops such as chopped corn or grass were compressed and preserved by their own fermentation; the resulting silage was fed to cattle in winter. The silos were usually square or rectangular and had two major faults: they were hard to pack, and silage became moldy in the corners. The professor's new silo quickly became popular because it was airtight, packed well, and made superior silage. In no time at all it became known as the Wisconsin, or King all-wood, circular silo.[2]

41. Professor Franklin King did early research on round wood silos and in 1889 designed the first true-round barn. Undated photograph, courtesy of the State Historical Society of Wisconsin.

King's research convinced him that the circle was an ideal shape for the barn itself. In 1889, for his brother's farm near Whitewater, Wisconsin, he designed and built a true-round barn with a round silo at the center. His new plan was widely published in agricultural journals.[3]

Some New York farmers who were won over by the merits of a round silo made of wood nevertheless shied away from a true-round barn as being too hard to build; others remained skeptical of the soundness of barns framed with the new, thin "dimension" lumber, 2" x 4" and 2" x 6" beams, the so-called balloon framing.

One New York State farmer compromised by putting a round silo in the center of his new timber frame octagon barn. Another put the silo in the center of his twenty-one-sided timber frame barn. Two others adopted both the center silo and balloon framing but stuck to the polygonal configuration: one farmer's barn was sixteen-sided and the other's was fifteen-sided.

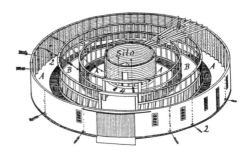

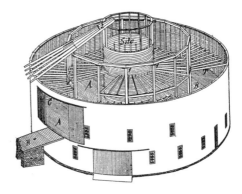

42. Franklin King's original true-round barn, built in Whitewater, Wisconsin, in 1889. From the Seventh Annual Report of the Agricultural Experiment Station, University of Wisconsin.

Octagon Barn in Oneida County

Near the Oneida County village of Holland Patent, an octagon barn was built in about 1890 on a road subsequently named Round Barn Road. Neither the name of the builder nor the original owner is known; the only documentation was a photograph from the Holland Patent library. The barn was located on Great Lot No. 173 of the Holland Patent. The Oneida County atlas for 1874 lists the owner as M. Tiernan, and the 1907 atlas lists a Mrs. E. Clark.

Jack Grogan rented the farm for nine years, from 1934 until 1943, and milked forty cows in the barn. He told me the barn was timber frame: "She was well built. She was pegged." In the center was a wood silo twelve feet in diameter and forty feet high. "If you didn't think it was a little trick to fill that!" he said. "But it was handy to feed once you got it full because the stanchions was all in a circle around the silo with the cows' heads facing in, and hay was handy to feed from the three hay chutes in the ceiling around the

43. This octagon barn, built around 1890 near Holland Patent, Oneida County, on a road later named Round Barn Road, had the first known round wood silo in New York State. Undated photo from the bicentennial book of Holland Patent, courtesy of the Preservation Center, Holland Patent Free Library.

silo."[4] (At corn harvest time in September, it took "tricky" maneuvering to place the belt-driven ensilage cutter on the outside haymow ramp where it would be both accessible to the wagons hauling cornstalks from the fields and suitably positioned to angle the discharge pipe to reach the top of the silo.)

There were three horse stalls in one section of the stable. A litter carrier for manure rode on a metal track suspended from the ceiling behind the cows. In the hayloft was a circular metal track for unloading hay from the wagons.[5]

This barn is significant because it is the first known instance of a round wood silo in New York State. Up to this time, silos on New York farms had been square structures with mortared stone walls.[6] The Holland Patent barn is doubly significant since it is the first known structure demonstrating the transition from haystack barn to central silo barn in this state. The acceptance of the central silo was crucial to the final phase in the evolution of the central plan barn.[7]

Hager-Gamel Sixteen-Sided Barn

Charles Hager was an Erie County, New York, farmer who trusted balloon framing and liked the idea of a wood silo in the center, but preferred the sixteen-sided barn plan over true-round. In 1901 he built such a barn at his farm on Shirley Road, about two miles south of the village of North Collins. In 1948 the farm was sold to the Maynard Gamel family.[8] Wayne Gamel continued the dairy operation into the 1980s.[9]

The barn is about eighty feet in diameter, two stories high with board and batten siding, and has a three-pitch gambrel roof, originally covered with wood shingles. In 1965, those were replaced with asphalt shingles. Clarence Kader, the carpenter who did the reroofing, said: "Mr. Gamel called me and said he wanted a new roof on his barn. When I got to look at the barn I was surprised to see it was round. I had a time figuring out how to figure it, so I figured out how much one of the 16 sides [of roof panels] would take and multiplied it by 16 giving me the number of squares required. I took the job by contract and ended up with $1/_4$ of a square left. I was a small contractor and worked alone after getting a scaffold on the roof. Mr. Gamel put the

44. The Hager-Gamel sixteen-sided barn, built in Erie County in 1901, features a unique three-hipped gambrel roof and a hay dormer. Photograph by Richard Triumpho, 1999.

shingles on the hay hoist and pulled them up with his tractor to the peak of the barn. I was a much younger man then. I am 90 years old now and it seems good to look back on some of the things I did."[10]

On the ground floor there are two windows in each of the sixteen wall sections. A large dormer is on the south side of the first roof level; it has double doors and a projecting track for hoisting hay. Both straight and circular hay fork tracks are hung in the loft.

A round wooden silo is in the center of the barn. It is surrounded by a circular feeding aisle, then the circle of stanchions for the cows, and finally the outside aisle or barn floor drive.

The Gamel barn is unusual in that it uses a flat site and does not have a ramp for bringing hay wagons into the loft. Instead, like many midwestern barns in similar flat situations, it solved the problem of hay storage by using a roof dormer and a system of hoists and hay tracks to lift hay up into the mow.[11]

Flanagan Twenty-One-Sided Barn

New York State's most northerly polygonal barn was located in St. Lawrence County in the town of Stockholm. In 1910 Charles Flanagan built a twenty-one-sided barn on the Southville Road between Routes 11 and 11B. It was a two-story timber frame barn, eighty feet in diameter, with a center silo sixteen feet in diameter and forty-six feet high. The barn had a stone foundation and was built on a level site, with two ramps to the hayloft.[12]

A distinctive architectural feature was a clerestory about three feet high. It had windows on every other wall section. The silo projected about four feet above the roof of the clerestory, and there were four windows evenly spaced around the top of the silo wall.

The silo was framed with 2" x 4" and 4" x 4" studs. It was double-walled with 3/8-inch elm boards, soaked in water and bent. The inside wall was then covered with lath and plaster. Iron hoops circled the silo. The metal roof was capped by a metal cupola built by Maxfield and Needham, a hardware store in Potsdam.[13]

45. The Flanagan twenty-one-sided barn, built in St. Lawrence County in 1910, had a clerestory. Photographer and date unknown.

The barn's ground-floor plan was circular, with forty-five cow stanchions facing the silo. Three of the twenty-one sections were taken up by horse stalls; one section was for calf pens. The flooring of the second story was two-inch plank.

Harold Flanagan took over the farm at the age of sixteen when his father, Charles, died. During the Great Depression, most of his herd was condemned during an outbreak of bovine tuberculosis that was controlled through a test-and-slaughter program, and Harold subsequently lost the farm. J. H. Dibble acquired the farm and continued to use the round barn for dairying until 1962. The barn fell down in the spring of 1999.[14]

Schultz Fifteen-Sided Barn

The last polygonal barn to be built in New York State is located in Sullivan County about one mile south of the village of Cochecton. It was built for John C. Schultz at his dairy farm along the northeast side of the Delaware

46. The Schultz fifteen-sided barn in Sullivan County, built in two phases in 1918 and 1929, proved that the round form could be adapted successfully to a smaller farm. Photograph by Richard Triumpho, 1998.

River. The barn was built in two phases: the first phase was done in 1918, and the second phase was completed in 1929.[15]

The barn is one and one-half stories high and has fifteen sides. It is balloon framed with 3" x 6" studs on a concrete foundation. Two sections of the ground-story wall, against the ramp to the loft, are concrete; the rest of the ground-story wall and the upper-story walls are sided with horizontal shiplap. There are wide entrance doors on the northwest and southeast sides. The nine other sides each have two pairs of windows.

The wood stave silo, bound with iron hoops and capped with its own gable roof, projects about twelve feet above the low-sloping conical roof of the barn. On the ground floor, the wood stanchions and the manger are in a circle facing the silo. A circle of posts around the silo supports the upper floor. Some of these posts carry up into the loft and support the roof rafters against the silo wall.

In the second story, the roof plate holds the rafters six feet above the loft floor; at the silo the rafters are twelve feet above the floor. The rafters are 3" x 6" beams on forty-inch centers at the wall. The roof has board sheathing covered with standing-seam tin, which is now covered with rolled roofing paper. The loft floor is boards over radial joists.

The Schultz family stopped dairying in 1986. The barn is now used to store farm implements.[16]

6 | Circles Within Circles

The central plan barn reached a higher stage of evolution with the wide acceptance of Franklin King's design: a circular barn of balloon framing with a cylindrical wood silo in the center.[1]

Voorhees Round Barn

New York State's first barn of this type was built in 1895 in Montgomery County by William H. Voorhees. He owned a milk bottling plant and milk delivery business in Amsterdam along with his dairy farm. Voorhees apparently saw King's plan either when it was first published in the *Seventh An-*

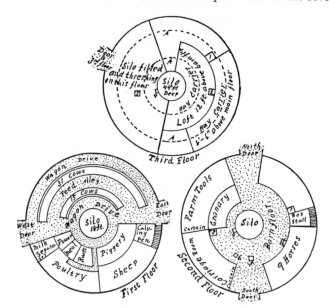

47. The Voorhees barn plan as printed in *Hoard's Dairyman*, March 26, 1897, from a letter sent by W. H. Voorhees to Professor King.

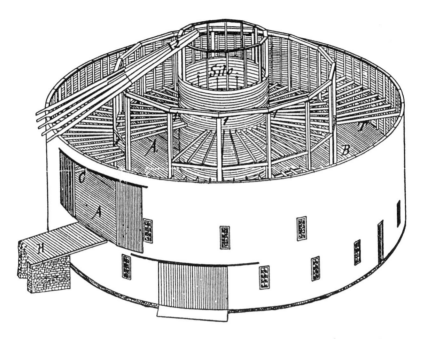

48. Voorhees barn elevation as printed in *Hoard's Dairyman,* March 26, 1897.

nual Report of the Wisconsin Agricultural Experiment Station or when it was reprinted in other farm journals;[2] he was completely captivated by the design and decided to build one like it.[3]

After Voorhees finished building his barn, he sent the floor plans and photographs of it to Professor King. The professor included the photographs in a letter to W. D. Hoard, and editor Hoard published the letter on the front page of his March 26, 1897, issue. King wrote,

> This barn possesses so many features of real merit, and so well illustrates a type of *consolidated farm buildings,* where all of the work in caring for farm stock may be done under one roof, that your readers will be glad to learn the results of Mr. Voorhees' efforts in producing a cheap, commodious, and convenient structure to fill the place of a large number of farm buildings.
>
> It will be seen from the two photo-engravings and the three floor plans that this barn is a three story structure, built in a country where the

topography makes it possible to drive with a team upon each of the three floors. The barn contains at its center a silo, 18 feet in diameter and 44 feet deep, which last year was filled to within one foot of the top. This filling is done from the third floor by driving there with the corn; and on the same floor, as shown on the plan, grain may be stored and threshed, the grain passing to the granary, directly below, and the straw to the scaffold where it may be stored ready for feed or bedding as desired.

This barn provides accommodations for forty-six cows, together with a separator room, power room, meal bins and calving pen. A wagon may be driven behind all of the cattle in cleaning the stable, and green feed in the summer may be delivered, by team to either end of the feeding alley or be driven through it. To accommodate these forty-six cows as here provided for, would require a barn not less than 44 x 70 feet on the ground, and the silo in this case would need to be a separate structure outside of the 44 x 70 feet. Mr. Voorhees' barn has a diameter of 88 feet.

In addition to this very conveniently arranged barn, Mr. Voorhees has, under the same roof, a barn for nine horses with box stall, and horse stairway leading to the floor below, together with storage for hay and grain, its floor space being equivalent to a structure of 20 x 50 feet.

He also has a sheep barn with root cellar and storage for hay and grain equivalent to a floor space 18 x 38 feet, and root cellar 11 x 12 feet.

Associated with the cow, horse and sheep is a poultry house 14 x 38 feet, and a piggery 12 x 34 feet. Under the same roof, too, there is a carriage and sleigh house, with floor space 18 x 37 feet, a house for farm tools with floor space equal to 18 x 46 feet, and a granary 12 x 30 feet.

Besides the accommodations enumerated, there is a large driveway on the second floor from which hay may be unloaded upon two circular tracks, the wagon standing at A A A on the third floor, the tracks being shown by dotted lines. These tracks are hung to the rafters close to the roof.

This barn encloses 253,416 cubic feet of space, and of this 60,262 cubic feet are available for the storage of hay, straw and grain, while 9,988 cubic feet of silage may be put into the silo.

The barn has been erected in a very substantial manner, slate being used for the roof; and nearly the whole of the basement has a cement floor, while metal conductors convey away the water from the roof. The floor above the basement is three inches thick; first, one inch boards, then paper, and then two inch planks. The two thicknesses of lumber and the paper were added for warmth in the stables below. So, too, the first two stories are both sheeted and sided, with paper between, for the first story.[4]

49. Built in Montgomery County in 1895 by William Voorhees, this was the first true-round barn built in New York State. Courtesy of *Hoard's Dairyman*. Photograph by William H. Voorhees, 1896.

50. When the Voorhees round barn burned down in 1944, a concrete round barn replaced it. Pride of ownership is evident in the crenelated wall. Photograph by Richard Triumpho, 1993.

Voorhees' barn became so well known in the Mohawk Valley that highway officials in the town of Glen renamed the road on which the barn was located "Round Barn Road."

Zoller-Fraiser Round Barn

Within a year after the Voorhees barn was completed, a similar barn was erected just thirty miles west up the Mohawk Valley in Herkimer County. It also closely followed Franklin King's model. The barn was built for Jacob Zoller on his dairy farm in the town of Danube on Fords Bush Spur Road, about two miles east of the hamlet of Newville. Zoller was also a pioneer food processor with a canning factory in Little Falls.[5]

The barn was two stories high and about eighty feet in diameter. It was constructed of balloon framing on a low foundation of mortared fieldstone. The wall siding was clapboard; the conical roof had wood shingles. An earth

51. This picture of the roof framing of the Zoller-Frasier round barn, built around 1896 in Herkimer County, shows its center silo and circular wooden hay track. Photograph by Richard Triumpho, 1993.

52. Roof framing of the
Zoller-Frasier barn.
Photograph by Richard
Triumpho, 1993.

ramp to the south met the hayloft entrance bay, which had wide double
doors and a modified gambrel roof.

The ground floor had a circle of stanchions around the central silo. The
silo was framed with 2" x 8" studding and rose up to within ten feet of the
cupola. There were wooden ladders nailed to the outside of the silo and
three small access doors at different levels.

The roof of the barn was built of 2" x 6" rafters radiating from the
cupola. The rafters had intermediate support from a circular purlin, which
in turn was supported by a heavy hexagonal plate of eight-inch-square
beams held by six squared posts with short diagonal braces. A circular
wooden hayfork track was hung from the rafters.

The round cupola was sheathed in wood shingles and had six combina-
tion louver and window openings. Its roof was a flared cone, demonstrating
a pride of workmanship that is characteristic of these barns.

53. The Zoller-Frasier round barn on its last legs, being pulled apart by a faulty foundation wall. Photograph by Richard Triumpho, 1993.

The barn had a beautiful setting situated on a bluff overlooking the Mohawk Valley and surrounded by open meadows on all sides.

In 1984, at the time of the Central Plan Dairy Barns of New York State Thematic Resources Survey, the barn was still being used in the dairy farm operation of the Frasier family. The survey listed it as being in fair condition. The accompanying photographs, taken in 1993, show how much it deteriorated in nine years. Four years later Blair Frasier took the barn down.[6]

Kelly Round Barn

Four years after Jacob Zoller built his circular barn in the Mohawk Valley, another barn based on Franklin King's prototype sprang up further to the south, in a valley along the east branch of the Delaware River.

In 1899 the Kelly brothers, Norman and George, began construction of a round barn on their farm near Halcottsville in Delaware County. The building was designed by Jason Whimple and built by Henry Sanford as mason and Asel Sanford as carpenter.[7]

The barn was about ninety feet in diameter, two and one-half stories high. This half-story, or attic, held a unique feature: a plank bridge that allowed teams to draw wagons from an east hillside entrance at the second story clear over the top of the hayloft and top of the silo. The bridge was supported by the top of the silo, and also by two interior bents with 8" x 8" posts. Arthur and Witney show a photograph of a round barn at St. Benoit-du-Lac, Quebec, which has a similar bridge but no silo.[8] The Erpf Catskill Cultural Center's "Historical Report" records that the Kelly brothers "went up to Canada one year on a cattle buying trip and as the story goes, they saw a round barn and decided to build one for themselves."[9] Could it have been the St. Benoit-du-Lac barn they saw?

The balloon framing of the Kelly barn had 2" x 8" studs on the ground floor and 2" x 4" studs at the upper level. Both stories were covered with shiplap siding. The roof's original wood shingles were covered with asphalt shingles.

On the ground floor the cows were in a circular ring of fifty-one stan-

54. The original Kelly true-round barn, built in 1899 in Delaware County. Courtesy of Valerie Voorhees.

55. Stable in a reproduction of the Kelly barn built by the Erpf Center. Photograph by Richard Triumpho, 1993.

chions facing the silo. In the stanchion ring were 3" x 8" posts, thirty inches on centers, supporting a header that carried 3" x 8" joists set radially. The aisle around the perimeter contained the gutter and drive floor.

The silo wall on the ground floor was a "sandwich" framed with 3" x 6" studs, sixteen inches on center, and covered outside with horizontal boards and inside with vertical tongue-and-groove boards. At the upper level the silo was framed with 3" x 4" studs and had exterior board siding only halfway up.

One innovation of the barn's wall framing was a laminated top plate of 1" x 4" boards bent to the round shape and sitting in let-ins to form a sandwich with the studs.[10]

In 1915, Chester Meade bought the farm and continued dairying until 1963. In 1981, Alta Industries purchased the Meade property; in 1986 Alta donated the barn and four surrounding acres to the Erpf Center, which planned a restoration project. By this time the barn had deteriorated so much that it was necessary to dismantle it. It was completely rebuilt, reusing as much material as was salvageable; unusable pieces were replaced with replicas. The restored barn now contains a Catskill museum and cultural center focusing on the region's agricultural tradition.[11]

56. John Anderson, Jr., the "Adirondack Lumber King," built a true-round barn in the late 1800s not, like most, to house cattle but to house his draft horses. Undated photo from *A History of Newcomb*.

Anderson Round Barn

All the true-round barns in New York State were built for dairy cattle with one exception. That one was built by a lumberman in the heart of the Adirondack Mountains. In Essex County in the town of Newcomb, John

57. Closeup view of Anderson's round barn in Newcomb, Essex County. Undated photograph courtesy of Patricia J. LaRocque.

58. Undated photograph of Anderson's round barn showing its setting in the heart of the Adirondacks. Courtesy of Virginia Hall, Newcomb Historical Society.

Anderson, Jr., was known locally as the "Adirondack Lumber King"; he built the barn to stable the eighty-five draft horses used in his extensive lumbering operations.

There is no firm construction date for the barn. The only information available comes from a few brief sentences in a book written by his great-granddaughter, Lana Fennessy: "John J. Anderson's round barn was a showplace of its day. It is no longer a feature of the town of Newcomb. The famous round barn was erected during the latter part of the 19th Century and was destroyed by fire in the fall of 1943." [12]

Stringham Round Barn

Dutchess County had the most unusual representation of a circular barn to be found in New York State. Around 1910 a rectangular barn owned by Varick Stringham, Sr., near Wappingers Falls, burned down in a fire, with the loss of many dairy cows as well as horses. When he rebuilt that same year was he determined to prevent a similar calamity in the future; he decided to sep-

59. Varick Stringham's concrete round barn even had a concrete silo, here being raised higher. Built about 1910 in Dutchess County, the barn was intended to protect his dairy herd from fire. Undated photo courtesy of Varick Stringham, Jr.

arate the cows from the hay. Stringham built a new, single-story barn about fifty-five feet in diameter with walls of poured concrete and a galvanized metal roof. In the center of the barn he erected a silo, also of poured concrete; it was better than forty feet high with a diameter of sixteen feet.[13]

Thirty-six cows were stanchioned in a circular ring around the silo with their heads facing in toward the manger and the six-foot-wide aisle surrounding the silo. The outside aisle behind the cows held the gutter and

60. This aerial view of Varick Stringham's round barn shows the adjoining two-story rectangular barn used for hay storage. Undated photo courtesy of Varick Stringham, Jr.

drive floor. About twenty-four windows, spaced evenly along the concrete wall, provided plenty of light inside.

A separate, gambrel-roofed rectangular barn was built for hay storage. However, the dairy operation was terminated sometime in the 1940s, and the circular concrete barn was torn down about 1950.[14]

Martinsburg Round Barn

In 1909, on a farm near the eastern fringe of the village of Martinsburg in Lewis County, Dr. M. Anstice Harris built a circular dairy barn. In the center was a round wooden silo that rose about twelve feet above the steeply sloping, truncated cone of the barn roof; the silo also had a conical roof, surmounted by a round cupola capped by another conical roof.

The barn held forty head of cows, stanchioned in a circle around the silo. The dairy had a trained farm manager and had every modern convenience of the time. It joined the small group of superior dairies in Lewis County authorized to ship certified milk to the New York City milk market. In 1918, however, hard times in the farm economy after World War I forced

61. The Martinsburg round barn, built in 1909 in Lewis County. Undated photo from archives of the William H. Bush Memorial Library.

the owners into bankruptcy, and the round barn was left vacant for several years. By 1965, a *History of Lewis County 1880–1965* recorded the owner to be Kate Greorezek, who kept a few cows and calves in the barn.[15] The barn burned either in 1992 or 1993.[16]

The Summit

Although Franklin King's circular barn plan was very popular, it did have some detractors. A chief complaint was with his conical roof, which required a structure of interior posts to carry the load; these posts seriously hampered the work space in the hayloft.[17]

Several Indiana barn builders improved on King's design by replacing the conical roof with a self-supporting gambrel roof, which left the mow space completely unobstructed.[18] In 1908 the Agricultural Experiment Station at the University of Illinois chose the gambrel roof style for three barns the dairy department built on the campus at Champaign. In 1910 the Experiment Station published the plans and building instructions in a bulletin, *Economy of the Round Dairy Barn*, which was widely distributed in agricultural circles.[19] The New York State circular barns built after 1910 reflect the influence of this Illinois bulletin in their choice of the gambrel roof.

Willsey Round Barn

Archie D. Willsey and his father, William Willsey, had a dairy farm on Switzkill Road about two miles south of the village of Berne in the rolling Helderberg hills of Albany County. Their herd of thirty registered Brown Swiss placed them among that breed of progressive dairymen who kept up with the new developments that were reported in agricultural journals. In addition to animal husbandry skills, both men were competent carpenters and cabinet makers.

They got the idea for a round barn from an article in the *Rural New Yorker*, which reprinted plans of the 1910 Illinois bulletin.[20] They began construction in 1912 and finished the following year.

Much of the lumber used for the new barn was salvaged from the old

62. The Willsey round barn was built in 1913 in the town of Berne, Albany County. This picture from 1931 shows Archie Davis Willsey and his children, Janis and Morris, in front of the barn. Photo courtesy of Morris Willsey.

barn they took down in March 1912. The new circular barn was sixty feet in diameter and sixty feet high. It was built *without* a silo in the center. Concrete for the foundation and floor was mixed by hand and contained creek

63. The Willsey round barn in 1972. Photo courtesy of Morris Willsey.

64. Morris Willsey, shown here in 1999, milked registered Brown Swiss in the round barn his father and grandfather built. Photograph by Richard Triumpho.

gravel. The sill and plates were sawed round on a table saw. The studs were thirty-eight feet long, all one piece.[21]

Only half of the first floor was used as the cow stable. In this section there were thirty-two metal stanchions arranged in a semicircle, facing the center. The stanchions and stall dividers were made by Louden, a farm equipment manufacturer in Fairfield, Iowa, and were set in place when the concrete was poured.

Instead of a cupola, the gambrel roof had a six-foot opening with a hinged cover in the center of the top. The roof was covered with wood shingles in time to store the summer hay harvest in 1912. The barn siding, put on after haying, was basswood boards, later covered with galvanized metal. The large doors to the hayloft were made curved to fit the barn. Morris Willsey, Archie's son, retired from dairying in 1962. Thereafter the barn was used for storage of his antique tractors. The barn burned down in 1997.[22]

Young Round Barn

In 1914, when James Clifford Young's barn burned near the village of Greene in Chenango County, he hired DeVern Bates to build a new one. Bates obviously was familiar with the circular barn designs widely promoted in the agricultural press at the time, for he designed a structure very similar to the plans published in the University of Illinois Agricultural Experiment Station bulletin in 1910.[23]

Bates built the barn over a period of two years. It is a two-story barn, about eighty feet in diameter. It has a conical double-pitched roof topped with a circular cupola containing louvers to vent the haymow and silo. The ground-floor framing is with 2" x 8" studs on a concrete foundation; the upper story is 2" x 6" studs; all sixteen inches on centers. The board siding is covered with pressed iron imitation brick sheathing. The roofing is standing-seam tin.

The central silo rises from the ground to the roof and is concrete-walled in the stable, but in the loft it is framed with 3" x 4" studs that are covered in-

65. James Clifford Young of Chenango County had this true-round barn built in 1914–15. Photograph by Richard Triumpho, 1993.

66. Stable in the Young barn, showing circular tie stall configuration and posts supporting the upper floor. Photograph by
Richard Triumpho, 1993.

side with horizontal boards and wrapped halfway up the outside with
beaded horizontal siding.

There are forty-seven tie stalls in a circle around the silo, with a manger
in front and a gutter behind. Originally, above the gutter was a track for a
manure carrier; it was replaced sometime in the 1950s by a circular, me-
chanical gutter cleaner. At the same time, the milk house was updated with a
bulk tank, and a circular stainless steel milk pipeline was suspended above
the cow stalls.[24]

Posts supporting a circular beam are spaced evenly around the stall circle. Another ring of eight posts (8" x 8") is spaced evenly around the silo;
these posts carry laminated beams (2" x 10" beams spiked together) that
form an octagon to carry the floor load around the silo. The joists are covered by a homosote ceiling, but their framing is assumed to be radial.

In the second story, 10" x 10" posts, in a circle directly over the first story
tie stall circle, rise to the break point of the roof. The aisle between this circle
and the silo is framed into a hayloft, with heavy beams between the posts
and the silo at the level of the wall plate. The outer aisle is open and used for
machinery storage.

The loft floor is two layers of boards laid perpendicular to the radially aligned joists. A large entrance bay with a gambrel roof faces the highway.

The roof is framed with 2" x 6" rafters. Two circular hay tracks are suspended from the rafters, one over the inner aisle and one over the outer aisle.

This is a handsome barn, well-designed and well-lighted by ample windows in the first story.

Bates Round Barn

Twelve years after DeVern Bates built the round barn for James Young, he decided to build one for himself on his farm near Greene, just a mile or so from the Young farm. He obviously kept well informed of new developments in Midwest barn-building circles, for his structure clearly shows the influence of the so-called Iowa barn plan. This final innovation used vitrified clay tile walls for the barn and silo instead of wood. Research on clay structural tile was done at the Iowa Experiment Station at Ames, hence the name.[25]

67. Bob Bates and his son outside the barn Bob's father built in Chenango County between 1928 and 1931. Courtesy of Bob Bates, 1993.

Bates began work in 1928 and finished in 1931 with a truly elegant barn. Built of concrete and structural tile, the three-story barn (with a fourth-story attic loft) is sixty feet in diameter and fifty-six feet high. The walls of the first two stories are tile. The third-story wall is framed with 2" x 6" studs and sided with clapboards, which later were covered with asbestos shingles.

The dome roof also has asbestos shingles over board sheathing. The roof was framed with curved, laminated rafters, three feet on centers at the wall. The rafters are five 1" x 4" boards nailed together after being bent to the proper curve. The tile silo rises through all three floors and the attic.

The floor of the loft is supported on the silo and outside walls; intermediate support comes from steel rods attached from the top of the silo to the midpoints of the floor beams and also from four kingpost trusses.

A major reversal of the ground-floor configuration has the cows in a circle of twenty-four stanchions facing the *outside* wall, with the manger in a wide aisle around the perimeter, and the gutter along the center aisle. This arrangement gave the cows access to better light and ventilation. Another in-

68. The Bates three-story barn with its vitrified tile walls was modeled closely on barns in the Midwest. Barn builders were always striving for improvements. Note the ventilating tubes on the outside wall. Photograph by Richard Triumpho, 1993.

69. Bob Bates and a cow in the Bates stable, designed so that the cows, in a stanchion ring, faced the outside wall for better light and ventilation. Photograph by Richard Triumpho, 1993.

novation is ventilating tubes along the wall to provide better air movement for the cows.[26]

The flooring of the second story is thin concrete over boards. This level has been used both for calves and chickens.

Since the barn is built against a hillside, the third floor has a large, level entrance bay with a pointed-arch roof. The entrance bay has a sophisticated facade comprised of an elliptically arched doorway with flanking lunettes and a round window at the center of the ogivally arched pediment.

The pediment surface is stucco, and door and window openings are handsomely headed with brick arches and surrounds. "Brook Haven 1931," lettered in brick within the stucco, gives a final artistic flourish to the facade.[27]

The Second Voorhees Round Barn

The first William Voorhees round barn, erected in Montgomery County in 1895, burned down in late summer of 1948. The cause of the fire was thought to be spontaneous combustion of damp hay. In 1950 the Voorhees built another round barn to replace it, this one only one story high and without a haymow. A separate barn was built for hay storage so that in the event of another fire, the cows would not be in danger.[28]

7 | Decline and Fall of the Round Barn

Round and polygonal barns enjoyed only a few decades of popularity before critics began unraveling what had been considered a superior design. By 1910, debate in the agricultural press over the advantages and disadvantages of these barns was being "fought with the ferocity and verbosity of opposing evangelists," according to Roger Welsch, who also noted that he had the distinct impression that most negative comments came "from theoreticians, while those farmers who live with the round barns are generally enthusiastic about them."[1]

Welsch came to this conclusion after reading the results of an agricultural experiment station questionnaire sent to 120 owners of round barns, which found that "no users reported dissatisfaction arising from the arrangement of their barns. They were unanimous in declaring them economical in construction and convenient in feeding and caring for stock."[2] Lowell Soike came to the same conclusion after he found "no instances of adverse comment" from owners.[3] One of the major faults cited by theoreticians was that the barn interior, being too far from windows in the outside walls, was poorly lighted and ventilated.[4] They recommended more windows and a central ventilator, which all the New York barns (with one exception) have. Indeed, the twenty-one-sided Flanagan barn in northern New York even had a clerestory, much like the famous Shaker round barn.

Even Professor Franklin King's innovation of locating the silo in the center of the barn came under attack in 1916 as being "inconvenient for filling" (and this from his original place of research, the Wisconsin Agricultural Experiment Station).[5]

The criticisms all seem unwarranted, given the fact that farmers who actually owned round barns continued to praise their efficiency. But this reversal of attitude from an agricultural press that had once proclaimed the virtues of the central plan dairy barn made many farmers in New York, as

70. The Flanagan twenty-one-sided barn in St. Lawrence County, depicted in a 1988 painting by Dorothy L. Goodrich of Brasher Falls, New York.

well as the Midwest, shy away from wanting to build one. Yet another hurdle to round barn construction was that carpenters and farmers were accustomed to straight lines and right angles; the circular form required skills that many carpenters simply didn't have.[6] Given these stumbling blocks, the wonder is that even forty-three were built in New York State. Obviously, the farmers who built them thought the advantages outweighed the disadvantages. Why then weren't more built during the late 1920s and beyond?

According to Soike, "Hard times sealed the fate of the round barn." The depressed farm economy in the 1920s, following World War I, and the Great Depression of the 1930s brought farm construction to a virtual standstill. "By the time farmers could afford to build again (after the Second World War)," Soike comments, "round barns—and traditional barns generally—had ceased to be practical."[7]

When the economy boomed again at the end of World War II, technological advances in farm mechanization changed the rural landscape forever. The horse was put out to pasture and replaced by the tractor with its multitude of equipment. The round barn was admirably suited for the era of horses and manual labor; it could not accommodate big tractors with their front-end bucket loaders, which could barely fit inside a round barn, let alone turn around in one. And when modern technology made it practical for silos to be built away from the barn, with silage fed out mechanically in automated feed bunks, the silo in the center of a round barn lost its advantage. The round barn and the traditional rectangular barn gave way to architecturally nondescript pole barns wide enough for tractors to work in. Electric motors powering conveyors that could move hay and silage anywhere in the barn made the centralized layout of circular barns unnecessary.[8] The round barn soon became as outdated as other relics of a bygone age—the ten-gallon milk can and the sulky plow, tucked away in some forgotten corner of the farmstead, now gathering dust and cobwebs.

Standing idle, a barn slowly deteriorates. A farmer cannot justify the cost of repairing a building not in use, especially with money in tight supply as it often is in the roller-coaster agricultural economy, where maintaining positive cash flow is a perennial farm problem.

Repairing the roof of a barn is the biggest expense. The cost of reshingling the roof of a round barn can easily run $20,000 or more.[9] Once the roof starts leaking, the fate of the barn is probably sealed. Water from rain and snow soaks the interior frame members; the purlins rot and fall, letting rafters sag; before long the roof caves in and the walls collapse on the ruins. Sometimes before this happens, the barn poses such a danger that the farmer attaches a chain and pulls it down. In one way or another, by fire or decay, New York has lost twenty-nine of its once proud round and polygonal barns. Only fourteen remain.

Just one of the original round and polygonal barns built in New York State is in use today on an operating farm: the Bates round barn in Chenango County still has dairy cows. Seven other of these New York barns are standing empty because their dairy-farm businesses failed. Farm profitability, which could have saved many of these barns in the first place, was inadequately addressed in earlier years of preservation efforts, and when it was brought up, farm failures were blamed on "inefficient management," or "too small a size to be viable," instead of the real culprit, perceived by many to be a government "cheap food policy" designed to keep prices low in the supermarket at the expense of the farm sector.[10] This same policy fostered the growth of megafarms and hastened the demise of small family farms.

While documenting barns for this book in travels through the state, I was astonished at the numbers of vacant or abandoned farms, particularly in a once prosperous dairy region such as Delaware County. But the land is now idle, the houses and barns empty and slowly deteriorating. Our barns are now on the list of endangered species along with that other vanishing breed, the family farm.

8 | Preservation

New York, like other states, for too long a time has been negligent in recognizing the historical value of her few round and polygonal barns. The Central Plan Dairy Barns of New York State Thematic Resources Survey of 1984 identified twelve barns suitable for nomination to the National Register of Historic Places. Eleven of these twelve inventoried barns were listed in the National Register that same year. The nomination directly benefitted the Kelly round barn by qualifying it to receive historic preservation funds.

Regrettably, funds were not available to help preserve the other barns. Since then, three of the barns have gone: two fell down, and one was pulled down because it posed a danger to anyone going inside. They disappeared because the cost of maintenance fell on the shoulders of owners who could not afford the burden. Those barns are, however, as a result of the Peckham and Reinberger survey, "preserved" on paper for continuing reference in state and federal archives.

Ideally, preservation of historic round and polygonal barns would ensure their continued use as agricultural structures, but the fact is that many of these barns no longer fit with modern industrialized methods of farming. We are fortunate, therefore, that five of the round and polygonal barns have been saved by conversion to other uses. Three of these function in ways completely removed from their agricultural origins. The Hubbell thirteen-sided barn in Jefferson and the Sid Sautelle octagon barn in Homer are now antique shops, while the Stony Brook octagon on Long Island is a private residence.

In two notable instances, local historical societies came to the rescue of endangered barns. The Bronck thirteen-sided barn has been admirably preserved and maintained by the Greene County Historical Society as part of the homestead of Pieter Bronck. Since the society receives no sustaining public funds, it depends on volunteer effort, membership dues, gifts, and legacies.

The Erpf Catskill Cultural Center in Delaware County undertook the

71. Another round barn saved by rehabilitation is the Sid Sautelle octagon barn, built in Homer, Cortland County, in 1905. Once housing a circus animal ring in the ground story it is now an antique shop. Photograph by Richard Triumpho, 1999.

salvation of the Kelly round barn in Halcottsville. In 1985, as part of the thematic nomination in New York State, the barn was placed on the National Register of Historic Places. The New York State Council on the Arts funded a historic structure report that was prepared by architect James Johnson. The barn had deteriorated to the extent that it was in danger of collapsing. Alta Industries, which had purchased the farm, donated the barn and four acres of land to the Erpf Center in 1986. In 1987 the Erpf Center carefully dismantled the barn. The next six years saw the barn rise again with much lumber salvaged from the original structure; unusable parts were used as models for new ones to complete the project. The barn is now used by the Erpf people as a Catskill museum and cultural center with a focus on the history of the region and its agricultural heritage.[1]

Today, finally, there is hope for our few remaining round and polygonal barns: support now is available from two new preservation organizations: BARN AGAIN! and the New York State Barn Coalition.

BARN AGAIN! is a national program to preserve historic farm build-ings. Since it was launched in 1987 as a joint venture by the National Trust for Historic Preservation and *Successful Farming* magazine, BARN AGAIN! has provided advice on preservation techniques to an average of seven hundred barnowners each year. The program has helped individual farmers find cost-effective alternatives to tearing down the old barn and putting up a new building. They provide practical information on how to adapt historic barns to other farm uses, for livestock or for machinery and grain storage.[2]

The New York State Barn Coalition was formed in 1997 as a "collabora-tive program of statewide, regional and local organizations, agencies and in-dividuals that recognize the economic, historic, symbolic and aesthetic value of barns and outbuildings. The coalition is dedicated to increasing public awareness and promoting the appreciation, preservation, rehabilita-tion and reuse of older and historic barns. The coalition works toward pre-serving agricultural landscapes, revitalizing rural communities, and fostering pride in New York State's cultural heritage."

72. The 1870 octagon barn in Truxton, Cortland County, once served as a road-house. Travelers' horses were stabled in the basement. Photograph by Richard Triumpho, 1999.

And, at long last, our state is coming to the rescue of its remaining barns. In the fall of 1996, Governor George Pataki signed into law the Farmer's Protection and Farm Preservation Act, designed in part to preserve historic barns. The New York State Office of Parks, Recreation, and Historic Preservation worked with the Department of Taxation and Finance to develop the Historic Barns Tax Credit. In order to qualify for an investment tax credit equal to 25 percent of the cost of rehabilitating the barn, it must house farm equipment, livestock, or farm products; it must be an income-producing barn; it must be a certified historic structure, or it must have been built or placed in service before 1936; and the rehabilitation must not alter the historic appearance of the barn. The credit applies to projects started after January 1, 1997.[3]

A certified historic structure is one that is listed on the National Register. Register-listed barns built after 1936 *do not* qualify for the tax credit. For barns built before 1936 that are not listed on the State Register of Historic Places, the owner must self-certify the work on the tax form.

73. The Kelly round barn rebuilt in Delaware County, 1992. Photograph by Richard Triumpho, 1993.

Also in the Farmer's Protection and Farm Preservation Act is a section (unrelated to the Historic Barns Tax Credit) that enables local municipal governments to enact property-tax abatement programs to phase in the increased value of barns that are rehabilitated.[4]

Since barn preservation efforts and availability of funding are continually changing, for current information, the reader should contact either the New York State Office of Historic Preservation, the Preservation League of New York State,[5] or the National Trust for Historic Preservation.[6]

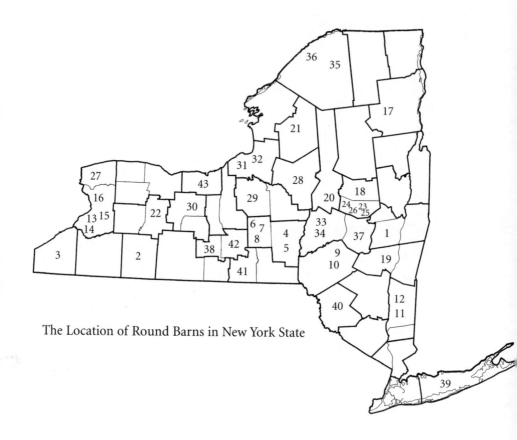

The Location of Round Barns in New York State

Catalog and Location of Round Barns

Albany County
1. True-Round Barn
Built: 1912–1913
Site: Town of Berne
Original Owner: William and Archie Willsey
Design/Builder: William and Archie Willsey
Photo: Morris Willsey 1960
Status: Burned

Allegany County
2. Nine-Sided Carriage Barn
Built: c. 1815
Site: Belvidere
Original Owner: Philip Church
Design/Builder: Unknown
Photo: Daniel Fink 1985
Status: Extant

Chautauqua County
3. Twelve-Sided Barn
Built: 1866
Site: Town of Westfield
Original Owner: Mr. Blowers
Design/Builder: Unknown
Photo: Donna Eisenstadt 1979
Status: Demolished

Chenango County
4. True-Round Barn
Built: 1914–1916
Site: Town of Greene

Original Owner: James C. Young
Design/Builder: DeVern Bates
Photo: Richard Triumpho 1993
Status: Extant

5. True-Round Barn
Built: 1928–1931
Site: Town of Greene
Original Owner: DeVern Bates
Design/Builder: DeVern Bates
Photo: Richard Triumpho 1993
Status: Extant

Cortland County
6. Octagon Barn
Built: 1902
Site: Town of Homer
Original Owner: Sid Sautelle
Design/Builder: Unknown
Photo: Richard Triumpho 1999
Status: Extant

7. Octagon Barn
Built: 1902
Site: Town of Homer
Original Owner: Sid Sautelle
Design/Builder: Unknown
No photo available
Status: Demolished

8. Octagon Carriage Barn
Built: c. 1900
Site: Town of Homer

Original Owner: Alphonso L. Head
Design/Builder: Unknown
Photo: Richard Triumpho 1999
Status: Extant

Delaware County
9. Sixteen-Sided Barn
Built: 1883
Site: Town of Kortright
Original Owner: John W. McArthur
Design/Builder: John Muir
Photo: Donald Martin 1984
Status: Demolished

10. True-Round Barn
Built: 1899
Site: Town of Halcottsville
Original Owner: Norman and George
   Kelly
Design/Builder: Jason Whimple
Photo: Richard Triumpho 1993
Status: Restored

Dutchess County
11. True-Round Barn
Built: c. 1910
Site: Village of Wappingers Falls
Original Owner: Varick Stringham Sr.
Design/Builder: Varick Stringham Sr.
Photo: Varick Stringham, Sr., c. 1910
Status: Demolished

12. Sixteen-Sided Chicken Barn Office
Built: c. 1900
Site: Washington Hollow
Original Owner: Unknown
Design/Builder: Unknown
Photo: None available
Status: Extant

Erie County
13. Octagon Barn
Built: 1874
Site: Town of Evans
Original Owner: Elliott W. Stewart
Design/Builder: Elliott W. Stewart
Photo: Town of Evans
Status: Demolished

14. Octagon Barn
Built: c. 1875
Site: Town of Evans
Original Owner: Elliott W. Stewart
Design/Builder: Elliott W. Stewart
Photo: Town of Evans
Status: Demolished

15. Sixteen-Sided Barn
Built: 1901
Site: Town of North Collins
Original Owner: Charles Hager
Design/Builder: Unknown
Photo: Richard Triumpho 1999
Status: Extant

16. Octagon Barn
Built: 1888
Site: Hamburg Fairgrounds
Design/Builder: Unknown
Photo: None available
Status: Extant

Essex County
17. True-Round Barn
Built: c. 1890
Site: Town of Newcomb
Original Owner: John Anderson Jr.
Design/Builder: Unknown
Photo: Postcard, undated
Status: Burned

Fulton County
18. Octagon Barn
Built: c. 1880
Site: Town of Ephratah
Original Owner: Levi Yauney
Design/Builder: Unknown
Photo: Unknown
Status: Demolished

Greene County
19. Thirteen-Sided Barn
Built: c. 1832
Site: Town of Coxsackie
Original Owner: Leonard Bronck, Jr.
Design/Builder: Unknown
Photo: Richard Triumpho 1994
Status: Extant

Herkimer County
20. True-Round Barn
Built: c. 1895
Site: Town of Danube
Original Owner: Jacob Zoller
Design/Builder: Unknown
Photo: Richard Triumpho 1993
Status: Demolished

Lewis County
21. True-Round Barn
Built: 1909
Site: Town of Martinsburg
Original Owner: Anstice Harris
Design/Builder: Unknown
Photo: Unknown
Status: Demolished

Livingston County
22. Octagon Barn
Built: c. 1860
Site: Town of Livonia

Original Owner: Unknown
Design/Builder: Unknown
Photo: Daniel Fink 1985
Status: Demolished

Montgomery County
23. True-Round Barn
Built: 1895
Site: Town of Glen
Original Owner: William Voorhees
Design/Builder: Unknown
Photo: Unknown
Status: Burned

24. True-Round Barn
Built: c. 1895
Site: Town of Minden
Original Owner: Unknown
Design/Builder: Unknown
Photo: None available
Status: Demolished

25. True-Round Barn
Built: 1950
Site: Town of Glen
Original Owner: Schuyler Voorhees
Design/Builder: Unknown
Photo: Richard Triumpho 1993
Status: Extant

26. Octagon Barn
Site: Fonda Fairgrounds
Built: Unknown
Design/Builder: Unknown
Photo: None available
Status: Extant

Niagara County
27. Octagon Barn
Built: c. 1880

Site: Hamlet of Ransomville
Original Owner: Unknown
Design/Builder: Unknown
Photo: Richard Triumpho 1999
Status: Extant

Oneida County
28. Octagon Barn
Built: c. 1880
Site: Village of Holland Patent
Original Owner: Unknown
Design/Builder: Unknown
Photo: Unknown
Status: Demolished

Onondaga County
29. Octagon Barn
Built: Unknown
Site: Syracuse Fairgrounds
Design/Builder: Unknown
Photo: None available
Status: Extant

Ontario County
30. Octagon Barn
Built: c. 1890
Site: Town of Seneca
Original Owner: Unknown
Design/Builder: Unknown
Photo: None available
Status: Demolished

Oswego County
31. Octagon Barn
Built: 1878
Site: Town of Hannibal
Original Owner: Unknown
Design/Builder: Orville Wiltse and W.
    H. Lund

Photo: Town Historian Archives
Status: Burned

32. Octagon Barn
Built: c. 1880
Site: Town of Mexico
Original Owner: John Williams
Design/Builder: Unknown
Photo: Town Historian Archives
Status: Extant

Otsego County
33. Octagon Barn
Built: 1882
Site: Town of Richfield
Original Owner: H. N., H. E., and N. R.
    Baker
Design/Builder: Probably the Bakers
Photo: Richard Triumpho 1993
Status: Extant

34. Octagon Barn
Built: 1885
Site: Town of New Lisbon
Original Owner: William Lunn
Design/Builder: Unknown
Photo: Richard Triumpho 1993
Status: Demolished

St. Lawrence County
35. Twenty-one-Sided Barn
Built: 1910
Site: Town of Stockholm
Original Owner: Charles Flanagan
Design/Builder: Unknown
Photo: Unknown
Status: Demolished

36. Octagon Barn
Built: c. 1871

Site: City of Ogdensburg
Original Owner: Oswegatchie
   Agricultural Society
Design/Builder: Unknown
Photo: None available
Status: Demolished

Schoharie County
37. Thirteen-Sided Barn
Built: 1896
Site: Town of Jefferson
Original Owner: Richtmeyer Hubbell
Design/Builder: Unknown
Photo: Richard Triumpho 1993
Status: Extant

Schuyler County
38. Octagon Barn
Built: 1893
Site: Town of Catharine
Original Owner: William S. Lattin
Design/Builder: George Stewart
Photo: Richard Triumpho 1999
Status: Extant

Suffolk County
39. Octagon Barn
Built: c. 1895
Site: Village of Stony Brook
Original Owner: Unknown
Design/Builder: Silas W. Davis
Photo: Beverly C. Tyler, Three Village
   Historical Society, 1999
Status: Extant

Sullivan County
40. Fifteen-Sided Barn
Built: 1918–1929
Site: Town of Cochecton

Original Owner: John C. Schultz (also
   the designer)
Design/Builder: Jacob Theis 1918, Louis
   Hocker 1929
Photo: Richard Triumpho 1998
Status: Extant

Tioga County
41. Octagon Carriage Barn
Built: Unknown
Site: Town of Newark Valley
Original Owner: Unknown
Design/Builder: Unknown
Photo: None available
Status: Extant

Tompkins County
42. Dodecagon Barn
Built: Unknown
Site: Dryden Fairgrounds
Design/Builder: Unknown
Photo: None available
Status: Demolished

Wayne County
43. Octagon Barn
Built: c. 1880
Site: Village of Red Creek
Original Owner: Burgess Jenkins
Design/Builder: Unknown
Photo: Daniel Fink 1985
Status: Extant

Notes

Preface

1. Larry T. Jost, *The Round and Five-or-More Equal-Sided Barns of Wisconsin* (Waukesha, Wis.: privately printed, 1980).

2. William L. Wells, *Barns in the U.S.A.* (San Diego, Calif.: Acme Printing, 1976).

3. Richard Triumpho, "Round Barns," *Agway Cooperator* (July/August 1993); and "Fondness for Barns Began in a Roundabout Way," *Country Extra* (July 1994).

4. Lowell J. Soike, *Without Right Angles: The Round Barns of Iowa* (Des Moines: Iowa State Historical Department, Office of Historic Preservation, 1983).

1. A Different Barn

1. John T. Hanou, *A Round Indiana: Round Barns in the Hoosier State* (West Lafayette, Ind.: Purdue Univ. Press, 1993).

2. For surges in barn construction in the Midwest, see Soike, *Without Right Angles,* 5.

3. This chronological order is from Mark Peckham and Mark Reinberger's survey, "The Central Plan Dairy Barns of New York State Thematic Resources" (Albany: New York State Division for Historic Preservation, July 1984), 7–12.

4. *Round* as a generic term was used by Roger Welsch in his article "Nebraska's Round Barns," *Nebraska History* 51 (1970): 49.

5. Eric Arthur and Dudley Witney, *The Barn: A Vanishing Landmark in North America* (Greenwich, Conn.: New York Geographic Society Ltd., 1972), 156.

6. According to Daniel Fink, when this type of framing, using light-dimension sawed lumber such as two-by-fours and two-by-sixes, was introduced in the 1830s, its detractors ridiculed it as being as insubstantial as a balloon *(Barns of the Genesee Country, 1790–1915* [Geneseo, N.Y.: James Brunner, 1987], 176).

7. Welsch, "Nebraska's Round Barns," 51.

8. Soike, *Without Right Angles,* 42.

9. Alfred Stefferud, ed., *Farmer's World: The Yearbook of Agriculture* (Washington, D.C.: United States Department of Agriculture, Government Printing Office, 1964), 8.

10. Hanou, *A Round Indiana,* 12.

11. Arthur and Witney, *The Barn,* 37.

12. Ibid., 44.

13. Ibid., 45.

14. Ibid., 69.

15. Ibid., 85.

2. Rounding Up Origins

1. Arthur and Witney, *The Barn,* 151.

2. Jost, *Round and Five-or-More Equal-Sided Barns of Wisconsin;* quotes on pages 1 and 3–5.

3. Arthur and Witney, *The Barn,* 147.

4. Ibid., 151.

5. Hanou, *A Round Indiana,* 4.

6. James Johnson and Diane Galusha of the Erpf Catskill Cultural Center and Mark Peckham and Mark Reinberger of the New York State Division for Historic Preservation all cite Walter William Horn and Ernest Born, *The Plan of St. Gall* (Berkeley: Univ. of California Press, 1979).

7. Philander D. Chase, ed. *The Papers of George Washington: Colonial Series* (Charlottesville, Va.: Univ. of Virginia Press, 1988).

8. *The Papers of George Washington* contains letters to Washington's agents in London, complaining about the low price he received for the tobacco he sent them, and the poor quality and high prices of the goods they charged to his account.

9. Witty Sanford, ed., *The Kelly Brothers Round Barn: An Historical Report 1899–1988* (Arkville, N.Y.: Erpf Catskill Cultural Center, 1988).

10. Sarah Booth Conroy and Adrian Higgins, "A Timber at a Time," *Washington Post,* September 19, 1996, 15.

11. From Sanford, *The Kelly Brothers Round Barn.*

12. Eric Sloane, *An Age of Barns* (New York: Ballantine Books, 1974).

13. Arthur and Witney, *The Barn,* 146.

14. It was described in the August 1831 *Genesee Farmer,* according to Fink, *Barns of the Genesee Country,* 369.

15. Greene County Historical Society archives.

16. This term was used as the title of a book about Orson Fowler by Carl Schmidt, *The Octagon Fad* (Scottsville, N.Y.: privately printed, 1958).

17. Randy Leffingwell, *The American Barn* (Osceola, Wis.: Motorbooks International, 1997), 100.

18. Welsch, "Nebraska's Round Barns," 58.

19. Arthur and Witney, *The Barn,* 147.

20. Ruby Rounds, ed., *Octagon Buildings in New York State* (Cooperstown: New York State Historical Association, 1954).

21. Soike, *Without Right Angles,* 6.

22. Welsch, "Nebraska's Round Barns," 58.

23. Fink, *Barns of the Genesee Country,* 370.

24. Ibid.

25. Ibid., 371.

26. Patterson Library archives. Westfield, N.Y.

27. Donna Eisenstadt, "Twelve-Sided Barn Is Crumbling," *Jamestown Post-Journal* (New York), January 19, 1979.

28. The photo was reported in Eisenstadt's article.

29. Mercy Nobbs Warren, letter to the author, August 1999.

3. A Flurry of Octagons

1. Soike, *Without Right Angles,* 11.

2. From the editorial page of the *Philadelphia Farm Journal* (February 1890).

3. "Faces and Places," *The Evans Journal* (undated clipping). Special thanks to Cheryl Delano and Donald D. Cook, Town of Evans historians, who found this clipping and a wealth of other information for me.

4. Ibid.

5. Soike, *Without Right Angles,* 10.

6. Ibid., 11.

7. Ibid.

8. "Faces and Places."

9. Soike, *Without Right Angles,* 10.

10. "Faces and Places."

11. Soike, *Without Right Angles,* 11.

12. "Faces and Places."

13. Peckham and Reinberger, "Central Plan Dairy Barns."

14. Ibid.

15. Ibid.

16. Susan Ferretti, letter to the author, March 5, 1998.

17. Ibid.

18. Harold J. Berry, Jr., interview with the author, June 8, 1999.

19. Ibid.

20. Bicentennial Historical Committee, *Our Todays and Yesterdays in the Town of Ephratah* (Ephratah, N.Y.: Ephratah Bicentennial Book Committee, 1976).

21. Lowell Newvine, letter to the author, July 21, 1999.

22. Helen M. Breitbeck, compiler, "Building Structure Inventory Form" (Oswego, N.Y.: Heritage Foundation of Oswego, November 22, 1983).

23. Helen Breitbeck, Heritage Foundation of Oswego; and Lowell C. Newvine, Hannibal town and village historian.

24. Larry Jost, from the list of Gene Sulecki, Rochester, New York.

25. Fink, *Barns of the Genesee Country,* 372.

26. Jost, from the list of Gene Sulecki.

27. Rodney Lightfoot, telephone interview with the author, July 14, 1999.

28. Peggy Holsten and Sidney Medd, "Building Structure Inventory Form" (Stony Brook, N.Y.: Three Village Historical Society, April 23, 1975).

29. Ibid.

30. Nancy Northrop, telephone interview with the author, August 12, 1999.

31. "Sid Sautelle Recalled," *Cortland Standard,* January 24, 1977. Thanks to the Cortland County Historical Society for tracking down this information.

32. Ibid.

33. Ibid.

4. Haystack Barns

1. Peckham and Reinberger, "Central Plan Dairy Barns."

2. John W. McArthur, *New Developments* (Oneonta, N.Y.: Oneonta Press, 1886), 139.

3. Ibid., 142.

4. Ibid., 143.

5. All descriptions of the electrical problems and the barn's collapse are from Donald Martin, interview with the author, July 18, 1999.

6. Martin, interview.

7. Quoted in Charles Hubbell, "Lucky 13," *Stamford Mirror Recorder* (Stamford, New York), June 2, 1988.

8. "Historic barns show weathered look," *Oneonta Daily Star,* November 4, 1985.

9. Peckham and Reinberger, "Central Plan Dairy Barns."

5. Circles in Polygons

1. The plans were published in the *Seventh Annual Report* of the Wisconsin Agricultural Experiment Station, and reprinted by the editor of *Hoard's Dairyman* in his April 19, 1895, issue.

2. Soike, *Without Right Angles,* 26.

3. Ibid., 29.

4. Jack Grogan, telephone interview with the author, July 17, 1999.

5. Grogan, telephone interview.

6. A stone silo is in the Baker octagon barn. My own 1874 English barn has an old rectangular silo of mortared stone.

7. Peckham and Reinberger, "Central Plan Dairy Barns."

8. Undated news clipping from Clarence Kader in a letter to the author, November 12, 1998.

9. Mrs. Wayne Gamel, telephone interview with the author, August 17, 1999.

10. Clarence Kader, letter to the author, October 30, 1998.

11. Peckham and Reinberger, "Central Plan Dairy Barns."

12. Dorothy L. Goodrich, telephone interview with the author, July 18, 1999.

13. Nola Collins, *The Round Barn* (Brasher Falls, N.Y.: privately printed, 1989).

14. Ibid.

15. Ed Schultz, interview with the author, October 24, 1998.

16. Schultz, interview.

6. Circles Within Circles

1. Peckham and Reinberger, "Central Plan Dairy Barns."

2. The plan was reprinted in 1893 by J. H. Sanders in *Practical Hints about Farm Buildings*; by the Chicago *Breeder's Gazette* both in its weekly journal and in its book, *Farm Buildings*; and by W. D. Hoard in the April 19, 1895, issue of *Hoard's Dairyman* (Soike, *Without Right Angles*, 29).

3. Albert Anderson said his two great-uncles, who dug the foundation for the barn, told him that the shale rock ledge had to be blasted, and that one dynamite charge never went off. The barn was built right over it anyway! (interview with the author, June 12, 1993).

4. *Hoard's Dairyman,* March 26, 1897.

5. Blair Fraiser, interview with the author, October 2, 1999.

6. Ibid.

7. From Sanford, *Kelly Brothers Round Barn.*

8. Arthur and Witney, *The Barn,* 156.

9. Sanford, *Kelly Brothers Round Barn.*

10. Peckham and Reinberger, "Central Plan Dairy Barns."

11. Sanford, *Kelly Brothers Round Barn.*

12. Lana Fennessy, *The History of Newcomb* (Newcomb, N.Y.: privately printed, 1996).

13. Varick Stringham, Jr., letter to the author, June 9, 1999.

14. Ibid.

15. G. Byron Bowen, ed., *History of Lewis County, New York, 1880–1965* (New York: Board of Legislators of Lewis County, 1970), 398.

16. Mrs. Howard Jantzi, telephone interview with the author, May 27, 1999.

17. Soike, *Without Right Angles,* 29.

18. Hanou, *A Round Indiana,* 15.

19. Soike, *Without Right Angles,* 29.

20. Morris Willsey, interview with the author, August 2, 1999.

21. Willsey, interview.

22. Ibid.

23. Wilber J. Fraser, *Economy of the Round Dairy Barn*, bulletin 143 (Urbana, Ill.: Univ. of Illinois Agricultural Experiment Station, 1910); Fraser, *The Round Barn,* circulation no. 230, revision no. 143 (Urbana: Univ. of Illinois Agricultural Experiment Station, 1918), 4–5.

24. Bob Bates, interview with the author, September 12, 1993.

25. Soike, *Without Right Angles,* 30.

26. Bates, interview.

27. Ibid.

28. Lynwood J. Hand, volunteer fireman, telephone interview with the author, August 14, 1999.

7. Decline and Fall of the Round Barn

1. Welsch, "Nebraska's Round Barns," 83.

2. Ibid.

3. Soike, *Without Right Angles,* 59.

4. *Hoard's Dairyman,* September 4, 1908.

5. F. M. White and D. I. Griffith, *Barns for Wisconsin Dairy Farms,* bulletin 266 (Madison: Wisconsin Agricultural Experiment Station, 1916); C. F. Doane, "Round Barns Not Practical," *Hoard's Dairyman,* February 20, 1914.

6. Soike, *Without Right Angles,* 60; Fred C. Fenton, "A Round Dairy Barn: Dairy Farmer Plan No. 9," *Dairy Farmer* (Des Moines), August 1927, 13.

7. Soike, *Without Right Angles,* 61.

8. Ibid.

9. Hanou, *A Round Indiana,* 60.

10. Martin Harris, Jr., "Northeast Opinion," *Farming: The Journal of Northeast Agriculture* (January 2000): 8–9; *Farming: The Journal of Northeast Agriculture* (December 2002): 10–11.

8. Preservation

1. From Sanford, *Kelly Brothers Round Barn.*

2. BARN AGAIN! 910 16th Street, Suite 1100, Denver, CO 80202. Phone (303) 623-1504. http://www.barnagain.org.

3. For information on the tax credit, contact the Business Tax Information Office of the Department of Taxation and Finance at (800) 972–1233, or the Preservation League at (518) 462–5658.

4. "Annotated Guide to Barn Preservation." Waterford, N.Y.: New York State Office of Parks, Recreation, and Historic Preservation, January 20, 1999.

5. New York State Barn Coalition, c/o Preservation League of New York State, 44 Central Avenue, Albany, NY 12206; telephone: (518) 462–5658 or (607) 272–6510.

6. National Trust for Historic Preservation, Northeast Regional Offive, Seven Faneuil Hall, Boston, Mass. 02109; telephone: (617) 523–0885.

Bibliography

Arthur, Eric, and Dudley Witney. *The Barn: A Vanishing Landmark in North America.* Greenwich, Conn.: New York Geographic Society, 1972.

Bicentennial Historical Committee. *Our Todays and Yesterdays in the Town of Ephratah.* Ephratah, N.Y.: Ephratah Bicentennial Book Committee, 1976.

Bowen, G. Byron, ed. *History of Lewis County, New York, 1880–1965.* New York: Board of Legislators of Lewis County, 1970.

Breitbeck, Helen M., compiler. Building Structure Inventory Form, November 22, 1983. Heritage Foundation of Oswego, Oswego, N.Y.

Chase, Philander D., ed. *The Papers of George Washington: Colonial Series.* Charlottesville, Va.: Univ. of Virginia Press, 1988.

Collins, Nola. *The Round Barn.* Brasher Falls, N.Y.: privately printed, 1989.

Conroy, Sarah Booth, and Adrian Higgins. "A Timber at a Time." *Washington Post,* September 19, 1996, 14–15, 18–21.

Cultivator and Country Gentleman (journal). 1854–1930. Albany, N.Y.

Fennessy, Lana. *The History of Newcomb.* Newcomb, N.Y.: privately printed, 1996.

Fenton, Fred C. "A Round Dairy Barn: Dairy Farmer Plan No. 9." *Dairy Farmer* (Des Moines), August 1927, 13.

Fink, Daniel. *Barns of the Genesee Country, 1790–1915.* Geneseo, N.Y.: James Brunner, 1987.

Fraser, Wilber J. *Economy of the Round Dairy Barn,* bulletin 143. Urbana: Univ. of Illinois Agricultural Experiment Station, 1910.

———. *The Round Barn,* circulation no. 230, revision no. 143. Urbana: Univ. of Illinois Agricultural Experiment Station, 1918.

Hanou, John T. *A Round Indiana: Round Barns in the Hoosier State.* West Lafayette, Ind.: Purdue Univ. Press, 1993.

Harris, Martin, Jr. "Northeast Opinion," *Farming: The Journal of Northeast Agriculture* (January 2000): 8–9; (December 2002): 10–11.

Hartman, Lee. "Michigan Barns, Our Vanishing Landmarks." *Michigan Natural Resources* 45 (1976): 17–32.

Hoard's Dairyman (journal). 1891–1920. Ft. Atkinson, Wis.

Holsten, Peggy, and Sidney Medd, compilers. Building Structure Inventory Form, April 23, 1975. Three Village Historical Society, Stony Brook, N.Y.

Horn, Walter William, and Ernest Born. *The Plan of St. Gall.* Berkeley: Univ. of California Press, 1979.

Jost, Larry. *The Round and Five-or-More Equal-Sided Barns of Wisconsin.* Waukesha, Wis.: privately printed, 1980.

King, Franklin H. "Plan of a Barn for a Dairy Farm," *Seventh Annual Report.* Madison: Univ. of Wisconsin Agricultural Experiment Station, 1890.

Klein, Howard. *Three Village Guidebook,* 2nd ed. E. Setauket, N.Y.: Three Village Historical Society, 1986.

Leffingwell, Randy. *The American Barn.* Osceola, Wis.: Motorbooks International, 1997.

McArthur, John W. *New Developments.* Oneonta, N.Y.: Oneonta Press, 1886.

Peckham, Mark L., and Mark Reinberger. "The Central Plan Dairy Barns of New York State Thematic Resources." Albany: New York State Division for Historic Preservation, July 1984.

Rounds, Ruby, ed. *Octagon Buildings in New York State.* Cooperstown: New York State Historical Association, 1954.

Sanford, Witty, ed. *The Kelly Brothers Round Barn: An Historical Report 1899–1988.* Arkville, N.Y.: Erpf Catskill Cultural Center, 1988.

Schmidt, Carl F. *The Octagon Fad.* Scottsville, N.Y.: privately printed, 1958.

Sloane, Eric. *An Age of Barns.* New York: Ballantine Books, 1974.

Soike, Lowell J. *Without Right Angles: The Round Barns of Iowa.* Des Moines: Iowa State Historical Department, Office of Historic Preservation, 1983.

Stefferud, Alfred, ed. *Farmer's World: The Yearbook of Agriculture.* Washington, D.C.: United States Department of Agriculture, Government Printing Office, 1964.

Stewart, Elliott W. *Feeding Animals: A Practical Work upon the Laws of Animal Growth Specially Applied to the Breeding and Rearing of Horses, Cattle, Dairy Cows, Sheep, and Swine,* 2nd ed. Lake View, N.Y.: privately printed, 1883.

Triumpho, Richard. "Fondness for Barns Began in a Roundabout Way," *Country Extra* (July 1994): 38–39.

———. "Round Barns," *Agway Cooperator* (July/August 1993): 16–17.

Wells, William L. *Barns in the U.S.A.* San Diego, Calif.: Acme Printing Co., 1976.

Welsch, Roger L. "Nebraska's Round Barns," *Nebraska History* 51 (1970): 49–92.

White, F. M., and D. I. Griffith. *Barns for Wisconsin Dairy Farms,* bulletin 266. Madison: Wisconsin Agricultural Experiment Station, 1916.

Worl, Gene. "Round Barns of Indiana." Indiana Room, Indiana State Library, Indianapolis, 1967–69. Photocopy of typescript.

Index